SpringerBriefs in Education

Key Thinkers in Education

Series Editor

Paul Gibbs, Middlesex University, London, UK

This briefs series publishes compact (50 to 125 pages) refereed monographs under the editorial supervision of the Advisory Editor, Professor Paul Gibbs, Middlesex University, London, UK. Each volume in the series provides a concise introduction to the life and work of a key thinker in education and allows readers to get acquainted with their major contributions to educational theory and/or practice in a fast and easy way. Both solicited and unsolicited manuscripts are considered for publication in the SpringerBriefs on Key Thinkers in Education series. Book proposals for this series may be submitted to the Publishing Editor: Marianna Pascale E-mail: Marianna.Pascale@springer.com

More information about this subseries at http://www.springer.com/series/10197

Paul Gibbs · Alison Beavis

Contemporary Thinking on Transdisciplinary Knowledge

What Those Who Know, Know

 Springer

Paul Gibbs
Azerbaijan University
Baku, Azerbaijan

Alison Beavis
Faculty of Transdisciplinary Innovation
University of Technology Sydney
Broadway, NSW, Australia

Faculty of Science
UNSW Sydney
Kensington, NSW, Australia

ISSN 2211-1921 ISSN 2211-193X (electronic)
SpringerBriefs in Education
ISSN 2211-937X ISSN 2211-9388 (electronic)
SpringerBriefs on Key Thinkers in Education
ISBN 978-3-030-39784-5 ISBN 978-3-030-39785-2 (eBook)
https://doi.org/10.1007/978-3-030-39785-2

© The Author(s), under exclusive license to Springer Nature Switzerland AG 2020
This work is subject to copyright. All rights are solely and exclusively licensed by the Publisher, whether the whole or part of the material is concerned, specifically the rights of translation, reprinting, reuse of illustrations, recitation, broadcasting, reproduction on microfilms or in any other physical way, and transmission or information storage and retrieval, electronic adaptation, computer software, or by similar or dissimilar methodology now known or hereafter developed.
The use of general descriptive names, registered names, trademarks, service marks, etc. in this publication does not imply, even in the absence of a specific statement, that such names are exempt from the relevant protective laws and regulations and therefore free for general use.
The publisher, the authors and the editors are safe to assume that the advice and information in this book are believed to be true and accurate at the date of publication. Neither the publisher nor the authors or the editors give a warranty, expressed or implied, with respect to the material contained herein or for any errors or omissions that may have been made. The publisher remains neutral with regard to jurisdictional claims in published maps and institutional affiliations.

This Springer imprint is published by the registered company Springer Nature Switzerland AG
The registered company address is: Gewerbestrasse 11, 6330 Cham, Switzerland

To those I love
—Paul

Acknowledgements

We are both very grateful for those who gave of their time in interviews to this project. Their status in Transdisciplinary arenas is well known whist their generosity of spirit perhaps less so.

We are also grateful to the team that have made the production of this publication possible, especially Alison Williamson and to the publisher Marianne Pascale for her support in bring this project to fruition. Finally our thanks go to Louise McWhinnie whose support both financially and emotionally has enable the project to come to realisation.

Contents

Part I Contextualisation

1 **Introduction to the Project** 3
2 **Transdisciplinary Knowledge—An Emergent Concept** 7

Part II The Interviews

3 **Sue L. T. McGregor** 19
4 **Valerie Brown** 25
5 **Gray Kochhar-Lindgren** 31
6 **Kate Maguire** 37
7 **Julie Thompson Klein** 43
8 **Linda Neuhauser** 53
9 **Basarab Nicolescu** 59
10 **Christian Pohl** 65

Part III Reflections and Case Study Appendix

11 **Thematics Reflections** 75

Appendix: Louise McWhinnie—My UTS Experience 79

Part I
Contextualisation

Chapter 1
Introduction to the Project

Transdisciplinarity today is characterised by its focus on 'wicked problems' that need creative solutions, a reliance on stakeholder involvement and engaged, socially responsible science. As a general perception, we would agree. Also, it has become common to discuss knowledge creation as co-produced, either under the rubric of an inter-, multi- or transdisciplinary mode of creation. Furthermore, in many cases, such pragmatic ways of dealing with problems have been undertaken without the insistence of academic rigour and, indeed, any insistence upon it has led to a degree of ridicule in practice-based occupations, whether justified or not. But academia has learned from the criticism of its ability to produce solutions to problems and to provide its graduates with the skills to engage in problem-solving—or at least some universities have! Such skills are not gained by drilling pre-work-based competencies but by a development of different ways of being in the world, ways that see a problem from many perspectives and can seek to resolve it within and outside the constraints that it presents. Certainly, such thinking has informed a recent and important form of assessment[1] of the ways in which UK universities set about doing their research, and success in doing this well will reap financial rewards.

There are also a growing number of academic degrees that suggest or actually deliver forms of a transdisciplinary curriculum, assessment and learning, conducted in collaboration with non-university entities. The number is not overwhelming, but is encouraging. One of the reasons for this, we believe, is an understanding of what stands behind all these developments: the notion of transdisciplinary knowledge has not been compellingly explored across the various approaches that dominate the literature. The purpose of this book is to explore this contested area, but not to solve it!

What is transdisciplinarity?

This is a straightforward question, but one that has proven rather difficult to answer compellingly. The emergence of transdisciplinarity (TD) has been in response to the often-failed attempts of closed-system, discipline-based approaches to solving

---

[1] For example, the 2020 Research Excellence Assessment evaluation.

complex social problems (various reports and definitions can be found in projects reported by the OECD, UNESCO and EU). We discuss in some detail in the following chapters both the history of transdisciplinarity and a number of its original thinkers. Indeed, UNESCO currently offers a definition of the transdisciplinarity approach to education as: 'An approach to curriculum integration which dissolves the boundaries between the conventional disciplines and organizes teaching and learning around the construction of meaning in the context of real-world problems or themes' (http://www.ibe.unesco.org/en/glossary-curriculum-terminology/t/transdisciplinary-approach). But to give us a work basis and to set a frame for the discussion in this book, we take (courtesy of the Faculty of Transdisciplinary Innovation, UTS[2]) its characteristics to be action oriented and focusing on addressing real-world complex issues:

It is participatory, considering not only scientific or academic knowledge but also forms of practical, local and personal knowledge.
It is continuously evolving in the 'pursuit of a common system purpose' (Jantsch, 1972).
In that process, it transforms and transcends individual disciplines.
It is holistic, building an understanding of whole systems and their complexity.
It is purposive, building a deeper understanding of a common human and social purpose to direct our efforts by bringing values and norms into play (Jantsch, 1972).

Such approaches need not be confined to large, seemingly insurmountable social problems, and may be applied equally well to issues within educational institutions as workplaces. The problems that transdisciplinary approaches tend towards are often complex and heterogeneous, specific, local and uncertain, epistemologically pragmatic and requiring ethically based practical action (Gibbs, 2015: 2). Yet, as we discuss, transdisciplinarity is more than a methodology grounded in conventional logics: it is an ideology; a disposition; a way of addressing the world in which one is emergent. As such, at its core, transdisciplinarity is transformative as well as a translational. However, knowing what something might feel like helps us to understand what it might be yet to leave gaps in how we might know it is. As De Santolo (2018) suggests, while talking about research within indigenous communities, which seems to pertain to all transdisciplinary research, our limitations lie in our inability to allow the research outcomes to transcend the heavily entrenched disciplinary silos within the academy. Disciplines tend to privilege different languages and processes, yet meaningful 'collaboration is vitally important if we are to overcome some of the systemic barriers to transformational change across different spheres of influence' (ibid: 215).

Transdisciplinary knowledge lies in the liberation of new and imaginative understanding from a notion of causality-predicated, discipline-ruled epistemologies within a closed system of the presenting problem. It is the understanding of the objects and structured reality of open social systems that gives rise to generative mechanisms, which are the cause of that to which we attribute the relationship of

---

[2] van der Bijl-Brouwer, M. https://futures.uts.edu.au/blog/2018/02/15/transdisciplinary-innovation-design/.

1 Introduction to the Project

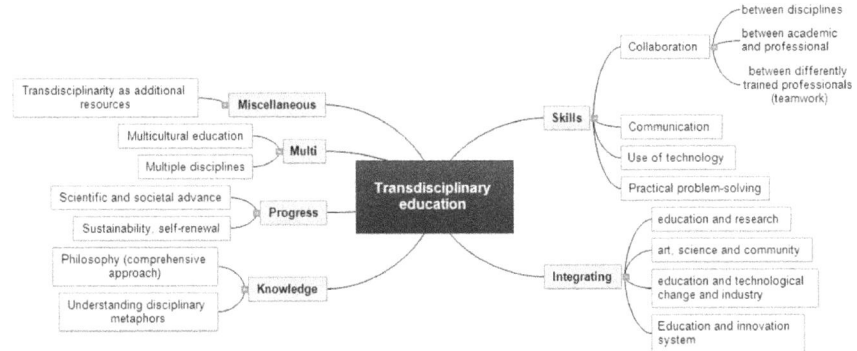

Fig. 1.1 Approaches to the concept of transdisciplinary education

agency and structure. How, then, might we understand what transdisciplinarity might actually be, given its complex and various uses? This book asks this question of leading practitioners in the field of higher education and transdisciplinarity.

Transdisciplinary education

The book tries to frame the transdisciplinary enterprise as an educative process through which people recognise their own complexity, incoherence and potential to become. The contribution of transdisciplinarity to higher education, in particular, is significant. The Fig. 1.1 gives some idea of how the concept has been addressed in studies conducted in 2018.

This figure illustrates the degree of complexity and the range of perspectives from which the concept has interested educational practitioners and researchers. These include discussions on synthesising case studies that facilitate collective learning and thinking across the fields of food security, sustainability, water planning, community engagement and public health, aiming to elicit a range of structural and conceptual designs for academic programmes at undergraduate, graduate and postgraduate levels. There are a number of higher education centres of excellence in research and teaching as transdisciplinary. The centres at ETH Zurich and the University of Texas are among the most well established as is the Faculty of Transdisciplinary Innovation at UTS. We have used the experiences of their Dean as a case study to highlight the issues that occur when adopting such a dedicated approach.

The book

To help to achieve this goal, we have gone to eight world-renowned experts in transdisciplinary research and practice. Their work is globally recognised, yet is not homogeneous: they develop, work and understand transdisciplinarity in different, worthwhile, insightful and exciting ways, and they often do this differently. That is not to say that there is no coalescence of thought and conceptualisation, and this we hope to review in the short studies that we have made of each of them in Chaps. 3–10. The selection comes from our appreciation of their work and from a desire to reflect a broad ideological (and geographic: European, Asian, Australasian and North American) background. We dedicate a chapter to each of these scholars in an attempt to capture how they understand transdisciplinarity in their practice. It is self-evident that we can do no more than offer a brief outline of their work and thinking, yet we have strived to capture sufficient of their approach to show their distinctive construction to our understanding of transdisciplinary knowledge. In these chapters, we hear from the featured scholars on: how thought style influenced Pohl's thinking; the centrality level of reality and resistance in Nicolescu's thoughts; Maguire's use of translation as a metaphor; McGregor's notion of knowledge as complex, emergent, embodied and cross-fertilised; Neuhauser's functionality; Kochhar-Lindgren's philosophical approaches; Brown's groundedness and Klein's pragmatics.

We then try, in the final chapter, to find the themes that run through these featured scholars' work. In this chapter, we do not try to create a uniform transdisciplinarity definition but to scope the terrain and its application to scholarship within what might be considered educational practice. We do this by discussing their views, so generously given to us in interviews, on the strongest themes that we identify in their work.

Finally, during these interviews there were a number of others who were identified as significant in the field. We offer the following list, but make no claim that those absent from it should not also appear: Gabriele Bammer, Alison Beavis, Matthias Bergmann, Josef Brenner, Paul Gibbs, Michael Gibbons, Donna Haraway, Gertrude Hirsch Hadorn, Roderick Lawrence, Helga Nowotny, Michael O'Rourke, Peter Osborne, BinBin Pearce, Patricia Rosenfield, Roland W. Scholz and Daniel Stokols.

References

De Santolo, J. (2018). Shelding Indigenous World From Extraction and Transformative Potential of Decolonizing Collabdtative Research. *Transdisciplinary Theory and Education, the Art of collaborative Resrach and collaborative learning* (pp. 203–219). Germany: Springer.

Jantsch, E. (1972). Towards interdisciplinarity and transdisciplinarity in education and innovation. In L. Apostell, G. Berger, A. Briggs, & G. Michaud (Eds.), *Interdisciplinarity: Problems of teaching and research in universities* (pp. 97–127). Paris: Centre for Educational Research and Innovation and OECD.

Gibbs, P. (2015) *Transdisciplinary professional learning and practice.* Springer.

Chapter 2
Transdisciplinary Knowledge—An Emergent Concept

Grounding of transdisciplinarity in its own history

This chapter seeks to present a concise overview of the history and knowledge of transdisciplinarity. It is not intended to be extensive but to set the scene for the interviews that follow. Readers are encouraged to explore alternative texts for a more comprehensive treatment of the topic (Augsburg, 2014; Klein, 2003, 2004, 2014). It is intended to contextualise the information from our key thinkers and provide a discussion of relevant contemporary themes.

The emergence of transdisciplinarity (TD) as a concept can be traced to the Organisation of Economic Cooperation and Development (OECD) International Conference on Interdisciplinary Research and Education in 1970. Influential researchers assembled in Paris to explore approaches to support universities in their quest to generate innovative solutions to society's challenges of the time. While interdisciplinarity was the focus of the seminar, TD was defined by a group of distinguished scholars using an axiomatic approach that transcends the narrow scope of disciplinary worldviews through an overarching synthesis. Three key researchers are generally attributed with leading the discourse: Jean Piaget, Erich Jantsch and Andre Lichnerowicz:

> Finally, we hope to see succeeding to the stage of interdisciplinary relations a superior stage, which should be 'transdisciplinary,' i.e. which will not be limited to recognize the interactions and/or reciprocities between the specialized researches, but which will locate these links inside a total system without stable boundaries between the disciplines. (Piaget, 1972: 144)

While Piaget and Jantsch positioned transdisciplinarity in terms of overarching systems and structures and patterns of thought, Lichnerowicz advocated for a common structure anchored in the deductive sciences of logic, utilising 'the mathematic' as a universal interlanguage (Lichnerowicz, 1972: 130–131). Jantsch described a multidimensional approach to education, structured as a multi-level and multi-goal system. Coordination was key element across the purposive, normative, pragmatic and empirical levels. He also emphasised a strong association of TD and social purpose:

> the essential characteristic of a transdisciplinary approach is the coordination of activities at all levels of the education/innovation system towards a common purpose. (Jantsch, 1972: 108)

We believe that this groundbreaking meeting in 1970 served to initiate significant future discussions, and the definitions by Piaget and Jantsch (Jantsch, 1970) are often claimed to be the most influential and widely cited (Augsberg, 2014). It is noted that Piaget was fully conscious of this alteration of transdisciplinarity, but the intellectual climate was not yet prepared for the shock of contemplating the possibility of a space of knowledge beyond the disciplines, with some suggesting that there had been a conscious decision to stage the evolution of the thinking. Ultimately, these seminal publications have helped to shape the subsequent divergence of ideas in the literature (Klein, 2004), although there is still a notion that 'transdisciplinarity remains "a rather elusive concept" that continues to evolve' (Jahn, Bergman, & Keil, 2012; see also Balsinger, 2004; Klein, 2004).

Contemporary themes

Divergence

As described previously, transdisciplinarity is often cited as lacking a common description. Here are multiple definitions and approaches (but it is arguably the Nicolescuian and the Zurich perspectives that feature most prominently (McGregor, 2015). The approach championed by physicist Nicolescu (2002) positions transdisciplinarity as a novel method to create knowledge aligned with three axioms, to be discussed below. The other, known as the Zurich approach, was formulated at the International Transdisciplinary Conference held there in 2000. At its core, it calls for the collaboration of experts from diverse fields on specific projects that transcend the boundaries of specific disciplines, conceptualising transdisciplinarity as an emergent form of research informed by the post-normal science perspective (Ravetz, 1999). In contrast to the Nicolescuian approach, the express intent is not the construction of new knowledge forms or realities.

Dispositions for transdisciplinarity

Another discourse that features prominently in the literature is the concept of a dispositional orientation to transdisciplinarity (De Freitas, Nicolescu, & Augsberg, 1994). Considerable discourse around transdisciplinary skills, characteristics and traits, as well as its virtues and practices, has been previously presented by Derry and Fischer (2005) and Mishra, Koehler, and Heniksen (2011). While these authors may present different sets of habits, dispositions and cognitive skills, there is a recognition that complex, wicked societal challenges demand perseverance, tolerance, creativity, insightfulness and a comfort with uncertainty (Costa & Kallick, 2008). Additional 'ideal qualities' include curiosity about, and a willingness to learn from, other disciplines, flexibility, adaptability, good communication and listening skills, and teamwork (Bruce et al., 2004: 464). Exploring specifically the skills necessary for academic research, Godemann (2008) identified the ability to look beyond one's own disciplinary boundaries, take on new ideas and reflect on knowledge integration processes and a capacity for disciplined self-reflexivity.

Additional research in exploring the cognitive tools that underpin TD approaches to thinking was conducted by Mishra et al. (2011). This work described seven habits of mind: perceiving, patterning, abstracting, embodied thinking, modelling, playing and synthesising.

The Politics of Disciplinarity

It can be argued that knowledge sits at the heart of every discipline, and knowledge, as we know, is power. By extension, at the heart of every discipline, then, is its *politics of knowledge production*. What constitutes knowledge? And, importantly, how do we evaluate the credibility of a claim to know? This concept will be explored in greater detail in both the interviews with key thinkers and later in this chapter.

It has been discussed that there is a 'growing acknowledgement of the internal complexity of the concept of an academic discipline, with often discrete intellectual, institutional and political aspects' (Osborne, 2015: 6). A key driver for the continuing dominance of the disciplinary approach in the university is the need for effective and efficient institutional structures for training students and facilitating an assembly of academics. By compartmentalising knowledge in separate disciplines, we risk being unable to 'recognize the inseparability of the separable' (Morin, 2006: 16). While disciplinary knowledge *can* be separated, any opportunity to address the open, networked and complex problems facing society will remain unrealised unless we reconceive of them as inseparable. Transdisciplinarity confronts the hegemony of disciplinary power, speaking truth to holders of powers, whether disciplinary elites, academic managers or policymakers. It challenges the knowledge culture and, as such, has at its core an educative purpose. We discuss this more later.

Considering knowledge

We live in a world that confounds simple analysis. It is a place in which things change and turn messy, where chance and causation are confused, and where truth and knowledge are empirical, perceptual or just faked. It is a world of many realities that is difficult to live in, and one where our own destructive history has led us to control rather than to reflect, appreciate, love or be humble. Academic disciplinary-based knowledge is fragmented, specialised, linear and scientific. It ignores or denigrates other forms of knowledge in its control of knowledge and truth. Many argue for new ways of envisioning knowledge and knowledge-creation practices, attributing the lack of any solution to our most pressing and fundamental problem, that of respect for our cosmos, to the structuring of knowledge into powerful silos and hierarchies. Moreover, these ways have a commonality in that they privilege abstract theoretical reasoning in certain acceptable paradigms. According to Foucault, the discipline principle is a 'principle which is itself relative and mobile; which permits construction but within narrow confines' (1981: 61). He continues:

> Still further: in order to be part of a discipline, a proposition has to be able to be inscribed on a certain type of theoretical horizon…. Within its limits, each discipline recognizes true and false propositions, but it pushes back a whole teratology of knowledge beyond its margins….

In short, a proposition must fulfil complex and heavy requirements to be able to belong to the grouping of a discipline; before it can be called true or false. (ibid: 60–61)

There is a mutual dependence between negative and positive functions here that characterises Foucault's conception of power and, congruent with that concept, it is misleading to focus on the negative functions alone: 'Foucault does not offer an anti-disciplinary stance with regard to academic disciplines in his critique of them, yet there is a tendency, in the direction of a loose transdisciplinarity, that nonetheless still runs through them'. Inter-, multi- and transdisciplinarity all depend upon the reproduction and development of the disciplines that they stand between, multiply or cross.

Knowledge is thus controlled by the powerful, and personal prudence prevents any permeation of ideas from discipline to discipline due to the impenetrable and artificial barriers of research practices, closed-belief systems, restricted vocabularies/grammars and the failure of collaborative conversations. So, while not denying the value of the focus of disciplinarity, it has become problematic in multiple and contested ways. It is in order to escape the constraints of disciplines on research, as 'limits to discovery' rather than as limits to freedom, that research has, de facto, increasingly become organised into interdisciplinary and often periodically reorganised project-based centres and, especially more recently, in policy-based, transnational, multi- and aspiringly transdisciplinary research organisations. It is in this context that the concept of transdisciplinarity has emerged and developed as a product of methodological self-reflection on new research processes.

Two approaches: One transcendent, the other recursive

Several approaches have been developed to answer the question of what knowledge is (its function, its constitution, its genealogy and its rationale) and, though parts of these theories are understood as useful for the task in hand, on their own they do not amount to a complete theory of knowledge and therefore of learning. These failures are often contingent upon disaggregated notions of knowledge (*gnosis*), turning into epistemology and ontology, creating an onto-epistemological narrative that is intent on informing practice but is often restrictive of freedom of thought, expression and innovation, which are the consequences of the ontological incongruities evident in discipline-based knowledge approaches. The need to change such knowledge positions applies equally well to the issues in emergent worlds that seemingly defy traditional, methodologically inspired empirical investigation.

Amid the boundary-spanning definitions of transdisciplinary knowledge that emerge from and are applied to transdisciplinary problems, any attempt to resolve value-laden issues requires judgement on the practical alternatives that affect others. They are not theoretical but practical, and are informed by the onto-epistemic principles contextualised in ethical and political contexts. These concerns are too important to be hampered by the constraints of disciplines and the forms of knowledge and the veracity that they sanction. The knowledge needed is both of the means to solve the problem and the goal of the solution. Knowledge is in the liberation of new and imaginative understanding from those meanings available under a notion of causality-predicated epistemologies within the closed system of the presenting problem. It is the understanding of the objects and the structured reality of open social systems that gives rise to the causal powers to which we attribute the relationship of agency and structure. It is in this sense that we explore knowledge that seems to us transformative—translational, as well as transdisciplinary—and with resonance with the claims that we make for the leaders in this academic field in this volume. We say academic, by way of acknowledging the many whose activities are not codified as transdisciplinary yet whose presence in a work of complexity of many other worlds and realities shows an agentic knowledge that is beyond this book.

As we have seen, concerns about the nature of transdisciplinary knowledge vary. As Mercier (2015) suggests, drawing on the work of Serres uncovers two principal transdisciplinary logics: one tied to idealities (abstract forms) and the other tied to the empirical domain (concrete information). For Serres (1974), 'transdisciplinarity' can also be described as a general theory and practice of translation, textual or empirical.[1] It provides opportunities to explore different ways of thinking through deep inquiry into complex world issues. The concept of transdisciplinary knowledge can be reviewed through two major and, perhaps, complementary orientations. According to the first, which has an epistemological and theoretical accent, transdisciplinarity is the process of knowing that which transcends disciplinary boundaries, and it entails a major reconfiguring of disciplinary divisions within a multi-reality, complex world. According to the second orientation, which is more pragmatic, participative and applied, transdisciplinarity can be thought of as a method of research that brings political, social and economic actors, as well as ordinary citizens, into the research process itself from a problem-solving perspective. Actors from outside the scientific field contribute to the construction of knowledge and solution of social problems that fall outside disciplinary boundaries. Transdisciplinarity is, perhaps, above all a new way of thinking about and engaging in inquiry. And transdisciplinary knowledge is created as a process of continuous refinement of multidisciplinary modes of knowledge aligned with features of the notion of Mode 2 knowledge (Gibbons et al., 1994).

The emergence initially created tensions in those institutions that may have profited from the decoupling of the forms of knowledge. Not least, this included universities that may have seen their mission to be the pursuit knowledge for its own sake, yet that are now recognising and actively embracing a more explicit economic role in the creation and transfer of knowledge. However, the dynamics of relationships and the forms of assessment of the nature of knowledge remain the same, even if the rational nature of the creator and use has become blurred. It embraces doing things differentially, not conceiving of the nature of knowledge in different multi-realities in a discontinuous form, in the way of being that we are ultimately comfortable with. Whereas Scott (2017) has argued for a discontinuity in the way in which we enframe disciplinarity and transdisciplinarity, in that to get from multi-mechanismicity to

---

[1] This separation coheres with the position taken by McGregor in this book; also, the notion of translation is central to the work of Maguire.

interdisciplinarity,[2] and thence to transdisciplinarity, we have to add considerations of emergence to those of complexity. A qualitatively new or emergent outcome is involved in the causal nexus at work, and then the knowledge required can no longer be generated by additive pooling of the knowledges of the various disciplines concerned but requires a synthetic integration, or genuine transdisciplinarity. If knowledge is understood as transdisciplinary, then its mode of production and its justificationary rationale are located outside those different academic disciplines altogether, and might be revealed in modes of truth that are dependent on poetics, metaphors and analogies, of folk knowledges and of the spiritual, mystical and profound.

We can thus draw a distinction between knowledge that is propositional (the kind of knowledge that we have when we know that something is the case), knowledge that is about processes (when we know how to do something) and what is sometimes referred to as knowledge with a direct object (when we know something or someone directly or through immediate experience). This might indicate that these forms of knowledge are fundamentally different, with strong and impermeable boundaries between them. As Scott (2017) suggests, this may be misleading. According to Papastephanou (2013), in addition to Aristotle's theory of knowledge as comprising of *theoria, poiesis, praxis*, there is textual evidence that he considered *khresis* (using) and *pathos* (passivity, receptivity or reactivity) as primarily complementary knowledge forms. Indeed, a transdisciplinary unification is possible, and is even indicated in Aristotle's gnoseology.

If we can accept this, then the highest level of all, transdisciplinarity, is framed in foundational terms and not, as might be stated, in some sense of an extension, completion or perfection of framings at lower levels—although one may have to go through the lower levels to arrive at the higher levels. This is a deeper understanding of being, of ourselves within the otherness of a presenting world, which may be outside the language of the rational. What this also means is that disciplinary knowledge, discipline-derived rationales for knowledge and discipline-based epistemic practices are, in some important ways, insufficient and undeveloped. The different levels necessary to the understanding of the result may be conceived as interacting or coalescing as a continuum or in a woven system of levels of reality.

The initial task then is to understand what transdisciplinarity knowledge might be. The premise here is that transdisciplinarity, monodisciplinarity, interdisciplinarity and disciplinarity constitute different forms of knowledge. A form of knowledge is constituted by its fidelity to certain types of norms, practices and protocols. Examples of these types include the accepted means for determining what is true knowledge in a community; the arbitration of good practice within the community over, for example, what constitutes quality; the semantic formulation currently in use; the type of values that are attached to concepts within the community and the types of power mechanisms that are in place to regulate these practices and protocols. For providers of education, their traditional role has been expressed in terms of producing autonomous individuals able to forge a self-sufficient way within a world,

---

[2] A Bhaskar (2016) term that embraces a multiplicity of causes, mechanisms and theories.

determined for the most part by their ability to grasp propositional knowledge. Might transdisciplinary knowledge be a space in which conceptual propositional knowledge is shared with activity-dependent concepts, revealed by engagement in the context of the action? It is where idealism and realism are realised, by many, for the first time.

To seek answers to these questions, in the next chapter, we explore the thoughts of the leading proponents of transdisciplinarity.

Transdisciplinary education

Education systems have been discipline based since the Middle Ages, whereby in the context of higher education universities were organised by academic disciplines such as medicine, law and theology. To accommodate the evolution of new knowledge, disciplines such as the physical and life sciences emerged in the nineteenth century and, a century later, in the social sciences. With curricula typically constructed around disciplinary structures, it is clear that disruption to such models has never been so necessary. In an address to the 2018 World Economic Forum, Justin Trudeau beautifully articulated this sentiment: 'The pace of change has never been this fast, yet it will never be this slow again'. The context of this statement relates to the need for radically different business models, yet it applies equally to education models. Today's students will move into a professional space dominated by new ways of working and jobs that did not exist when they commenced education.

Anchoring learning to standard disciplinary structures could be argued as limiting the agility needed for cross-disciplinary creativity to emerge. Considerable research suggests that students are challenged by transferring academic knowledge across fields and do not feel comfortable applying knowledge gained in one field to another, or to real situations. It is argued by McGregor (in Gibbs, 2017) that a TD curriculum facilitates the co-creation, co-dissemination and integration of transdisciplinary knowledges that emerge from the interaction between disciplines.

Transdisciplinary learning has been presented by Pohl et al. (2011) as possessing four features: (a) it relates to socially relevant issues, (b) it transcends and integrates disciplinary paradigms, (c) it involves participatory research and (d) it entails a deep search for a unity of knowledge. Such approaches to higher education are beginning to emerge globally, with a range of approaches from single, isolated learning experiences to degree-level education programmes.

References

Augsburg, T. (2014). Becoming transdisciplinary: The emergence of the transdisciplinary individual. *World Futures, 70*, 233–247.
Balsinger, P. (2004). Supradisciplinary research practices: History, objectives and rationale. *Futures, 36*, 407–421.
Bhaskar, R. (2016). *Enlightened common sense: The philosophy of critical realism*. Abingdon: Routledge.
Bruce, A., Lyall, C., Tait, J., & Williams, R. (2004). Interdisciplinary integration in Europe: The case of the Fifth Framework programme. *Futures, 36*, 457–470.

Costa, A. L., & Kallick, B. (2008). *Learning and leading with habits of mind: 16 essential characteristics for success.* Alexandria, VA: ASCD.

De Freitas, L., Morin, E., & Nicolescu, B. (1994). *The charter of transdisciplinarity.* Retrieved from International Encyclopedia of Religion & Science, http://inters.org/Freitas-Morin-Nicolescu-Transdisciplinarity.

Derry, S., & Fischer, G. (2005). Toward a model and theory of transdisciplinary graduate education. Paper presented at the American Educational Research Association Conference. Available at http://l3d.cs.colorado.edu/~gerhard/papers/transdisciplinary-sharon.pdf.

Foucault, M. (1981) The order of discourse. In R. Young (Ed.), *Untying the text: A post-structuralism reader* (pp. 51–78). London: Routledge & Kegan Paul.

Gibbons, M., Limoges, C., Nowotny, H., Schwartzman, S., Scott, P., & Trow, M. (1994). *The new production of knowledge: The dynamics of science and research in contemporary societies.* London, UK: Sage.

Gibbs, P. (2015) *Transdisciplinary professional learning and practice.* Springer.

Godemann, J. (2008). Knowledge integration: A key challenge for transdisciplinary cooperation. *Environmental Education Research, 14*(6), 625–641.

Jahn, T., Bergmann, N., & Keil, F. (2012). Transdisciplinarity: Between mainstreaming and marginalization. *Ecological Economics, 79,* 1–10.

Jantsch, E. (1970). Inter- and transdisciplinary university: A systems approach to education and innovation. *Policy Sciences, 1,* 403–428.

Jantsch, E. (1972). Towards interdisciplinarity and transdisciplinarity in education and innovation. In L. Apostell, G. Berger, A. Briggs, & G. Michaud (Eds.), *Interdisciplinarity: Problems of teaching and research in universities* (pp. 97–127). Paris: Centre for Educational Research and Innovation and OECD.

Klein, J. T. (2003). Unity of knowledge and transdisciplinarity: Contexts of definition, theory and the new discourse of problem solving. In G. H. Hadorn (Ed.), *Unity of knowledge (in transdisciplinary research for sustainability) (Vol 1)* (pp. 35–39). Paris, France: UNESCO EOLSS.

Klein, J. T. (2004). Prospects for transdisciplinarity. *Futures, 36,* 515–526.

Klein, J. T. (2014). Discourse of transdisciplinarity: Looking back to the future. Futures, 63, 68-74.

Lichnerowicz, A. (1972). Mathématique et transdisciplinarité. In L. Apostel, G. Berger, A. Briggs, & G. Michaud (Eds.), *L'interdisciplinarité: Problémes d'eseigment et de recherche, Centre pour la Recherche et l'Innovation dans l'Enseignement* (pp. 122–26). Paris: OCED.

McGregor, S. L. T. (2015) The Nicolescuian and Zurich approaches to transdisciplinarity. *Integral Leadership Review, 15*(2). Retrieved from http://integralleadershipreview.com/13135-616-the-nicolescuian-and-zurich-approaches-to-transdisciplinarity/.

McGregor, S. (2017). Transdisciplinary Pedagogy in Higher Education: Transdisciplinary Learning, Learning Cycles and Habits of Minds. In P. Gibbs (Ed.), *Transdisciplinary higher education: A theoretical basis revealed in practice* (pp. 3–16). Dordrecht: Springer.

Mercier, L. (2015). Introduction to Serres on transdisciplinarity. *Theory, Culture & Society, 32*(5–6), 37–40.

Mishra, P., Koehler, M. J., & Henriksen, D. (2011). The seven trans-disciplinary habits of mind: Extending the TPACK framework towards 21st century learning. *Educational Technology, 11,* 22–28.

Morin, E. (2006). *Restricted Complexity, General Complexity* (p. 16). Worldviews, Science and Us: Philosophy and Complexity.

Nicolescu, B. (2002). *Manifesto of transdisciplinarity* (K. C. Voss, Trans.). Albany, NY: State University of New York Press.

Osborne, P. (2015). Problematizing disciplinarity, transdisciplinary problematics. *Theory, Culture & Society, 32*(5–6), 3–35.

Piaget, J. (1972). L'epistémologié des relations interdiciplinaires. In L. Apostel, G. Berger, A. Briggs, & G. Michaud (Eds.), *L'interdisciplinarité: Problémes d'eseigment et de recherche, Centre pour la Recherche et l'Innovation dans l'Enseignement (pp 144).* Paris: OCED.

References

Papastephanou, M. (2013). Aristotelian gnoseology and work-based learning. In P. Gibbs (Ed.), *Learning, work and practice: New understanding* (pp. 107–120). Dordrecht: Springer.

Pohl, C. (2011). What is progress in transdisciplinary research? *Futures, 43*, 618–626.

Ravetz, J. R. (1999). What is Post-Normal Science. *Futures, 31*, 647–653.

Scott, D. (2017). Interdisciplinarity, transdisciplinarity and the higher education curriculum. In P. Gibbs (Ed.), *Transdisciplinary higher education: A theoretical basis revealed in practice* (pp. 32–44). Dordrecht: Springer.

Serres, M. (1974). Transdisciplinarity as relative exteriority. In *La Traduction: Hermès III* (pp. 152–157). Paris: Minuit (Trans. L. Mercier (2015). *Theory Culture and Society, 36*(5–6), 41–44).

Part II
The Interviews

Chapter 3
Sue L. T. McGregor

Sue McGregor is a Professor Emerita and Canadian home economist (over 45 years), recently retired from Mount Saint Vincent University, Halifax, Nova Scotia, Canada. She was one of the lead architects for the inter-university doctoral programme in educational studies, serving as its inaugural coordinator. She has a keen interest in home economics philosophy, transdisciplinarity and consumer studies. She is an ATLAS Fellow (transdisciplinarity), a docent in home economics at the University of Helsinki, a Marjorie M. Brown Distinguished Professor (home economics leadership), a Karpatkin International Consumer Fellow and she received the TOPACE International Award (Berlin) for distinguished international consumer scholarship. Affiliated with 16 professional journals (as editor, co-editor, associate editor and board member), she has written 200 peer-reviewed publications, 31 book chapters, 12 monographs and five books. She has delivered 30 keynote presentations and been invited to join talks in 14 countries. She is Principal Consultant for the McGregor Consulting Group (1991). She has written extensively on transdisciplinarity and, of her works, those we consider her most influential are: 'The Nature of Transdisciplinary Research and Practice' (2004), 'The Nicolescuian and Zurich Approaches to Transdisciplinarity' (2015), 'Transdisciplinary Knowledge Creation' (2017a) and 'Challenges to Transdisciplinary Collaboration: A conceptual literature review' (2017b).

We regard Sue's position on transdisciplinarity to be captured in this short summary:

> Sue frames the transdisciplinary enterprise as an educative process by which people become a more complex self as they engage in transdisciplinary work using the transdisciplinary methodology. In turn, this complex self, who has experienced a series of inner changes (paradigmatic, intellectual and philosophical), can better contribute to solving the problems of the world using the transdisciplinary methodology. Transdisciplinary knowledge creation helps participants grow into collaborative, complex

> problem-solvers. To develop this idea, her work introduces the concepts of *transdisciplinary self* and *transdisciplinary maturity*. For her, the genesis of transdisciplinarity is detailed in Basarab Nicolescu's transdisciplinary methodology.

The following are informed by an interview held with Sue in June 2018 when she was in Canada.

Can you briefly describe your intellectual relationship to transdisciplinarity?

Interesting question… It all started when I discovered that the UNESCO Commission for Canada was having its 2004 meeting in Halifax, NS (close to where I worked). I was then Coordinator of our university's Peace and Conflict Studies program. I asked and UNESCO agreed to let me attend their meeting. Once there, I discovered that the conference theme was transdisciplinarity (TD), which I'd never heard of before. I am home economics, which has always been interdisciplinary. After I attended the meeting, I began to research TD and wrote a paper about it once I felt I had sufficient understanding. It was published in a journal called *Kappa Omicron Nu Forum*, which is a home economics leadership journal. The paper was entitled 'The Nature of Transdisciplinary Research and Practice'. In effect, I serendipitously discovered TD when attending a UN conference and while learning more about it, I discovered Basarab Nicolescu's work. That's why everything I do now is based on his work, because that was my first orientation to TD.

In 2005, I received an email from Basarab commenting on that paper and telling me how good he thought the article was (*'an extraordinarily profound summary of TD'*); that I understood TD so well and explained it in plain language and used good metaphors. I was so in awe. And then I just kept on trying to figure out how he understood it and decided from then on that my role was to try to put TD in plain language so others can take up the idea. So, all I did from then on is try to understand the abstract nature of his models and their attributes and convey that in research articles. So my interest in TD started at a 2004 UN meeting and continues unabated 14 years later.

What does TD practice and knowledge mean to you?

I think it depends on which of the schools of transdisciplinarity you look at. Two approaches to transdisciplinarity tend to prevail: (a) the Nicolescuian approach and (b) the Zurich (Swiss) approach. If you go to the reference list of people's papers, you will usually see that they are citing sources for one or the other but not both. The Zurich approach is evident in citations for Nowotny, Klein and Gibbons. Familiarity with both approaches is recommended because each one yields different insights into the complex problems facing humanity. The Nicolescuian approach was developed and is espoused by Professor Dr. Basarab Nicolescu, a Romanian quantum physicist based in Paris, France. Starting in the late seventies, he 'worked out' a methodology of transdisciplinarity (with three axioms) and then strategically arranged for its dissemination in a series of books and congresses, the first being in 1994. The Zurich approach to transdisciplinarity stems from a March 2000 congress in Zurich,

Switzerland, co-organised by Roland Scholz. As an aside, those in attendance at the Zurich meeting were aware of Basarab's approach but opted to advance a different approach to transdisciplinarity.

To answer your question, the Nicolescuian approach assumes that TD knowledge is complex, emergent, cross-fertilised, embodied and alive. It is created in the fertile ground where disciplines and lifeworld actors meet to address wicked problems. Nicolescuian TD practice deeply involves reconciling contradictions and tensions among diverse actors as they employ inclusive logic and draw on as many perspectives (Realities) as possible. The Zurich approach assumes that the creation of TD knowledge involves the synthesis of existing knowledge available from disciplines and social actors. The resultant knowledge will be socially robust, reflexive and accountable. Zurich TD practice involves disciplines working with practitioners within social constraints—do science better. There is no concern for reality or logics.

Do you have a preference?

I have a longstanding interest in research methodologies (the creation of new knowledge) so I think I like Basarab's approach the best, because it's a new methodology. And I see it as a way to create knowledge, whereas in the Zurich school science is still the preferred methodology—you just need to 'do the science differently'. So, having thought about it more, I think the Zurich approach appeals to people because it gets them on the ground faster. They do not have to think about knowledge *creation* because they are synthesising *existing* knowledge and using it immediately. People think it is easier for people to comprehend and understand because the Zurich approach is more practical. Nicolescu described his approach to transdisciplinarity as theoretical and the Zurich approach as phenomenological meaning it is focused on 'application in context'. Diversity in approaches to transdisciplinarity is desirable.

What do you think is distinctive about the creation of TD knowledge?

Again, I think it depends on which school you're in. The Zurich TD's school of thought pushes interdisciplinarity so all the sciences interact, but science is working with society to identify the problems and come up with solutions that are implementable right away. People perceive that solutions arise much faster and people hit the ground faster because that's the intent (i.e. application in context). Your background is disciplinary; you just have to think differently about how to use your background so you can deal with complexity.

Basarab created a very different approach to the creation of TD knowledge calling it a new *methodology* with axioms: what counts as knowledge (complexity and epistemology), what counts as reality (multiple levels of Reality whose interaction is mediated by the Hidden Third) and what counts as logic (inclusive so it can include many perspectives, disciplinary and lifeworld). Approaching the creation of knowledge is very much based on philosophy. He came up with this approach back in the late seventies, I think, when he was in California. He was so rogue at the time, and risked his career trying to put this idea forward because he was just pushing the boundaries of everything at a time when positivism and empirical methodology reigned. I think he is rogue now too because he is advocating for an approach to knowledge creation that is predicated on the new science of quantum physics, complexity theory and chaos theory. Also, most researchers are familiar with the quantitative and qualitative (and mixed methods) approaches (methodologies) that are based on *assumptions*. But fewer people are comfortable with discussing philosophical *axioms* as they inform knowledge creation.

Can you give me a short description of how you envision Basarab's ideas on knowledge and reality?

He has very distinct ideas about knowledge and reality informed by the *new* sciences (complexity, chaos and quantum thought). My understanding is that TD assumes that there is tension between people's ideas, images and representations of reality and what these claim to represent. These tensions hold things together as they emerge and are referred to by Basarab as resistance. Reality (capital R) is defined as that which resists people's images of life. People involved in solving issues related to poverty, for example, each bring their own perspective to bear and it is natural to resist others' views. Their Reality pushes back. Nicolescu asserts that if Reality were merely socially constructed, a consensus of a collectivity, there would be nothing to resist. However, quantum physics allows people to resist the idea that Reality is tangible and concrete; they can now assume it is malleable and pliable and able to change. Embracing the idea of multiple levels of Reality, people can now co-create new images of Reality.

Appreciating that bringing disparate minds together would be inordinately challenging, Basarab conceived of the *Hidden Third*. By this he meant a force that mediates the interface between contradictory points of view. To explain, I now understand that Reality is something that people encounter that resists their current understandings of, or experiences in, the world. They can encounter this resistance in the environment, the economy and the cosmos (external world) and they can encounter this resistance in their inner world (their lived history, social connections, and their individuality and philosophy). To mediate and reconcile this resistance, they need the richness of religions, spiritualities and cultures/expressions of art—the sacred. He called this the Hidden Third.

Then, to be able to move from one reality to another (breakthroughs and new insights), Basarab holds that people need the logic of the included middle that says that things are in flux and alive with constant change and interactions; new knowledge is created as people move through the different levels of resistance. Nicolescu refers to this logic as the 'included middle' because, in contrast, Newtonian logic assumes that the space between things is empty, flat, static—a vacuum. This void does not merit attention. Worse—perceiving this space as empty means that many ideas fall between the cracks. Nicolescu creatively drew on the quantum notion of the vacuum as energy at its lowest level, ripe with potential. I think the axiom of the included middle is very powerful. This inclusive logic enables people to imagine that the space between things is alive, dynamic, in flux, moving and perpetually changing. It is in this fertile middle space that transdisciplinarity manifests because TD knowledge involves a marriage between the disciplines and civil society.

Whereas interdisciplinarity builds bridges among disciplines so people and ideas can cross back and forth (assuming that a bridge is needed to cross the deep, empty chasm), transdisciplinarity has people stepping onto the fertile middle ground. This involves moving through their zones of non-resistance to reach an area where people can then work together to generate new TD intelligence and knowledge, facilitated by the unifying Hidden Third.

I use the metaphor of a lava lamp to help people to understand that future realities are constantly in flux. The viscous fluid of the lamp is always in movement, with new things bubbling up and falling back onto those moving about on the undulating floor (the included middle). This embodied knowledge is created from the energy generated from intellectual and perspective fusion. When the separate bits of knowledge and the people who carry them came together to dance in the fertile transdisciplinary middle, they move faster when they are exposed to each other than when they are alone, creating intellectual fusion. Everyone *owns* the new knowledge.

Could you say a little more about the associated values that you see in transdisciplinarity?

I have had interesting email conversations with Basarab about this, and I actually met with him in Paris (the highlight of my academic life). We have agreed to disagree on the role of axiology (values) in TD knowledge creation. He thinks people's individual values matter less than the transdisciplinary values that emerge from interaction in the included middle. While respecting this, I also think that because transdisciplinarity is about understanding the problems of the world, those engaged in transdisciplinary work would be concerned with values because they are working together in fluctuating, enriching and challenging relationships. By their very nature, interactions among multiple actors give rise to value conflicts and contradictions that must be acknowledged and reconciled. These value conflicts can result in power struggles. In a TD approach, power is energy; it is *capacity* generated through relationships. Without relationships, there can be no power. Whether the power generated as people work together to solve complex, emergent problems is negative or positive depends upon the nature of the relationships. That, in turn, is predicated on values reconciliation. Furthermore, with power comes responsibility. I know Cicovacki (2009) makes a strong case for an axiology of transdisciplinary, as I have done in what I call 'integral value constellations'. I see it as the fourth axiom of transdisciplinarity.

Can we finally discuss barriers or challenges to the development of transdisciplinarity?

I have recently written about this in a paper entitled 'Challenges of Transdisciplinary Collaboration: A conceptual literature review'. Four overarching issues were identified: (a) managing group processes, (b) reflexivity, (c) the common learning process and (d) facilitating integration and synthesis. People engaged in TD work are wrestling with how best to ensure that collaborations among diverse actors accommodate the *special qualities* of transdisciplinary work. I do not think that Basarab writes much about this issue but the larger body of literature agrees that in order to have effective activities in an inclusive setting, the group has to work through an intensive and ongoing collaboration. This effort ensures they can adapt to the increasing complexity of their interactions. Actually, I was recently told that Basarab uses the term TD *hermeneutics* in reference to interpretation, understanding and meaning making among a disparate collection of stakeholders as they work collaboratively but I have not explored this construct in detail yet.

References

Cicovacki, P. (2009). Transdisciplinarity as an interactive method. *Integral Leadership Review, 9*(5). Retrieved from http://www.archive-ilr.com/archives-2009/2009-10/2009-10-06-article-cicovaki.php.

McGregor, S. L. T. (2004). *The nature of transdisciplinary research and practice*. Kappa Omicron Nu Human Sciences Working Paper Series. Retrieved from http://www.kon.org/hswp/archive/transdiscipl.html.

McGregor, S. L. T. (2015) The Nicolescuian and Zurich approaches to transdisciplinarity. *Integral Leadership Review, 15*(2). Retrieved from http://integralleadershipreview.com/13135-616-the-nicolescuian-and-zurich-approaches-to-transdisciplinarity/.

McGregor, S. L. T. (2017a). Transdisciplinary knowledge creation. In P. Gibbs (Ed.), *Transdisciplinary professional learning and practice*. Cham: Springer.

McGregor, S. L T. (2017b) Challenges to transdisciplinary collaboration: A conceptual literature review. *Integral Leadership Review, 17*(1). Retrieved from http://integralleadershipreview.com/15402-challenges-of-transdisciplinary-collaboration-a-conceptual-literature-review/.

Chapter 4
Valerie Brown

Emerita Professor Valerie Brown. Her careers as a prolific author, educator, researcher and policy expert have often been linked by one common feature—the blank canvas. She has been responsible for taking on numerous institutional, sector-wide and government initiatives to establish (from scratch) ways of knowing and doing. Her work on collective thinking defined a period of her scholarly output, but she has now moved beyond to explore Independent Thinking. From her perspective, human ideas and actions have led to unprecedented changes in the relationships between humans and between ourselves and the Earth. Changes in the air we breathe, the water we drink and the energy we use are evidence of Nature, which has no special interest in sustaining human life, looking out for itself. For humans to meet these challenges requires social reorganisation that is neither simple nor easy. An effective response will require independently thinking individuals working together.

Her profound contributions on independent thinking explores workable strategies from the frontiers of creating a viable future for humans on Earth, based on research results from hundreds of social learning workshops with communities worldwide, many of them part of the Australian National University's (ANU) Local Sustainability Project. The multiple dimensions of individual, social and biophysical ways of thinking are combined in ways that allow open-minded individuals to learn from each other. She has written extensively on transdisciplinarity and, of her works, those which we consider her most influential are the seminal *Tackling Wicked Problems: Through the Transdisciplinary Imagination* (2010), *Collective Learning for Transformational Change: A guide to collaborative action* (2012), and *The Human Capacity for Transformational Change: Harnessing the collective mind* (2014).

We regard Val's contribution to transdisciplinarity to be captured in her own words in the following abstract to her 2015 paper in *Future*:

> The future is frequently presented as a forced choice between human sustainability and human extinction, utopia or dystopia. This paper examines a different option: to develop the full capacity of the human mind to remain open to all possibilities, guided by utopian thinking. An inquiry into the creative potential of the human mind finds that collective thinking from a collective mind goes beyond transdisciplinarity as currently constructed. In collective thinking, knowledge boundaries are reframed as dynamic inter-relationships, and due weight is given to each of personal, physical, social, ethical, aesthetic, sympathetic and reflective ways of knowing. In applying the collective mind in these times of transformational change, there is hope for innovative solutions to seemingly intractable, aptly labelled wicked problems.

The following was with Val in Australia in November 2018.

Can you give a brief description of your relationship to transdisciplinarity, val?

I would never have called what I do transdisciplinary, and I don't now. If you wish to describe my relationship to transdisciplinarity, you could say 'I'm over it!'

My relationship to TD goes back to 1972, but you can imagine the word 'transdisciplinary' had not yet been heard. Even the concept of it was heresy. Given it was 1972, and naturally given the topic of my PhD thesis was 'Holism and the University Curriculum: Promise or performance', I certainly built on Piaget, who had just referenced transdisciplinarity in his essay. I was also fortunate to be exploring this topic at a time when scholars such as Foucault were writing his thesis, so I must be one of the very few people who actually read his preliminary work. It was inspiring, between Piaget and Foucault, and a lot of people may have found them because they were still on the edge of their own careers.

My thesis drew the conclusion that, while universities expressed the aim of addressing complex issues as a whole, in practice they remained strongly partitioned along disciplinary lines that were seen as essential for the university to function. I was told by the deputy vice-chancellor at the time that I was 'tearing the university down brick by brick'.

After completing my doctorate, I became involved as a course evaluator with the team led by Professor Steven Boyden and others, who were breaking the very boundaries I explored in my thesis. This helped to reinforce my perspective that the academic world was not like that. And what do you do then? My options at this point were to disseminate my thesis as a book in the traditional way or take another fantastic opportunity to lead the development of pioneering new programme at the University of Canberra. It was the first science degree in health education. This was one of my many experiences of being drawn to a blank slate.

My understanding of TD has also been shaped by many experiences, including my role as public health service director. My view of transdisciplinarity as beyond the disciplines and outside academia didn't change, but the context in which it was delivered did. While I didn't enjoy the same freedoms as developing and running programmes at Australian National University (ANU) and the University of Canberra, I learned so much, in one sense about transdisciplinarity. When we refer to 'beyond the disciplines' we must also include the public service. One must understand the organisational politics: the concepts of knowledge, even how knowledge itself is taken into account, and how it's integrated, how it's applied, how it's evaluated. It also provided a deep understanding of how deadly the disciplinary boundaries were. I'd stopped thinking they were just a limit or a bother, and saw them being actually deadly. It was mucking up social advance. It was mucking up people. I developed a real sense of purpose.

What does TD practice mean to you?

I would describe my approach to TD practice as simply not wanting to observe disciplinary boundaries. I've never believed in them. I've written a lot about transdisciplinary or whatever label is used. Now I'm writing about how the social rules impede the individual, which is quite a shift. They limit their own identity. But returning to transdisciplinarity, it's been difficult to convince people that the individual thinking was so different from the socially induced thinking that it's actually a different phenomenon. So the socially induced thinking is being called transdisciplinary. Yes?

So I've now somewhat moved on from transdisciplinary practice, which I'm now calling Independent Thinking. I've moved on from Collective Thinking and I've gone through Collective Thinking to Individual Thinking on the same basis, and I've now come out the other side and I'm doing what it takes to be an individual in a monopoly world. That's what TD practice means to me now, assuming that knowledge is only created in a human head, and so if there's an exemplar, then an independent individual that I'm looking at, and I've got some criteria, which I'll expand upon. This now means thinking for yourself, independently and being able to speak the language and move in the circles that are actually the society.

What criteria do you use to acknowledge TD as plausible knowledge?

I'm now arguing that, in the work we've done, we've identified ways in which individuals carve up knowledge. We've looked at how societies carve up knowledge, and we've been right because the response to that has been quite major. Of course, you can't avoid thinking like the society. But what I'm arguing is that has always been a corruption of how people think. If you look at the individual, we have, I believe, emerged in our work different dimensions. I'm calling it the multidimensional mind.

So, the five criteria or dimensions from my perspective. It's not psychology, it's not sociology. It's none of those things. It's sheer on-the-ground observations of what people do, right? And the programme I've been running, all through all of this, has involved workshops on transformational change with communities, so my observations are underpinned by considerable data. Individuals think, first of all, which isn't surprising, physically, bio-physically. But I don't mean like a discipline. They look for themselves. The second criterion relates to social. Thirdly—ethical, which is a good thing. Aesthetic. No question at all. And sympathy. They are intentional positioned away from disciplines.

So ultimately, what I've given you are the criteria I used to acknowledge, not transdisciplinary, but plausible knowledge.

Do you associate values with transdisciplinary, or TD knowing in ways that differ from other forms of knowledge?

If what I'm believing is right, then people doing TD are also using those five criteria I described in the previous question; perhaps they're just not acknowledging it. I've done some workshops on that, and that's very interesting. The workshops have explored what academics *think* they're doing. Actually, I'm writing up this particular workshop at the moment, and it's interesting. A social scientist, extremely well experienced and published, doing a major national project, happy with four of those ways, but one criterion upset him badly, and he wouldn't have it. Which one do you think? Physical? No. It was Aesthetic. He would not have it. 'Oh, what's it doing there?' 'No, no, I never use it. No, never'.

It's so interesting. Actually, he is very sympathetic and very, very good on the Social criterion. And so that, not only the Social, but he has the sympathy for his participants and his work. Yes. But that always fascinated me.

Who do you consider is shaping our understanding of TD?

There's always been somebody. Now, I think you do, because of its nature, you have someone. It is often a writer in literature rather than a real-life person. I mean, I live in books so, to me, I'd have to go into a long explanation why someone in a book can be even more real to me.

There are other important influences, such as Isaiah Berlin. I found him long ago, and now I absolutely would say it's Berlin, even though I've never met him. But the one I have met is Jerome Rivet. He is the authority on post-normal science. So, you know, it's great to talk to him because he's been there. He's going to write the foreword for an upcoming book I'm writing.

What allows TD to thrive?

I'll reflect by commenting on a chapter in one of my books called 'Walling In and Walling Out'. And one of the themes is how walls can keep you away from something, or walls can be a meeting place. And so, I'd comment on hurdles and ways that TD can thrive from this perspective, because ultimately, what's a hurdle?

I mean, I could answer socially constructed knowledges, easily. But no, the bit that's interesting to me is the section about, right, you've got a wall. What do you do with it? The 'Walling In and Walling Out' chapter is inspired by a Frost poem called *Mending Walls*. The poem explores two neighbours—one who views the walls as creating separation and security, while the other questions the need for the wall, seeing it as unnecessary:

He is all pine and I am apple orchard.
My apple trees will never get across.
And eat the cones under his pines, I tell him.

This is a lovely extension to the concepts of transdisciplinarity and the barriers that can often prevent it from thriving.

References

Brown, V. A. (2015). Utopian thinking and the collective mind: Beyond transdisciplinarity. *Futures, 65,* 209–216.

Brown, V. A., & Harris, J. A. (2014). *The human capacity for transformational change: Harnessing the collective mind.* London: Routledge.

Brown, V. A., & Lambert, J. A. (2012). *Collective learning for transformational change: A guide to collaborative action.* London: Routledge.

Brown, V. A., Harris, J. A., & Russell, J. Y. (2010). *Tackling wicked problems: Through the transdisciplinary imagination.* London: Routledge.

Chapter 5
Gray Kochhar-Lindgren

Gray Kochhar-Lindgren is Professor and Director Common Core, University of Hong Kong (HKU). Given the forces of globalisation, technology, migration and digitisation that are so powerfully shaping the contemporary university, such a reconfiguring of transdisciplinarity enables students to prepare more fully for the knowledge and experience economy, to make connections between their majors and other areas of learning and to begin to think about the meaning of ethics in the context of extremely complex dilemmas. He has also initiated Global Liberal Arts Design Experiments (GLADE) in order to create a space of exchange for those working on holistic learning in research-intensive universities. Professor Kochhar-Lindgren was previously appointed as the inaugural Associate Vice-Chancellor for Undergraduate Learning and Professor of Interdisciplinary Arts & Sciences at the University of Washington, Bothell. With degrees in philosophy, religious studies, literature and a PhD in Interdisciplinary Studies, Gray is the author of *Narcissus Transformed*, *Starting Time*, *TechnoLogics*, *Night Café*, Philosophy*, Art, and the Specters of Jacques Derrida*, and *Urban Arabesques*. Currently, he is working on collaborative projects on philosophy in the city and the emerging global university. The recipient of three teaching awards, most recently as the leader of the HKU Outstanding Teaching Award (Team) for *Transdisciplinarity-in-Action*. Gray has taught in Switzerland, Germany and the United States, and in 2009–10 served as a Fulbright Scholar in General Education at the University of Hong Kong. His work on the topic, which includes philosophical contributions on the nature of the university and the application of his work in the University of Hong Kong, is referenced at the end of this chapter.

We regard Gray's position on transdisciplinarity to be captured in this short summary:

> In building the Common Core and HKU, Gray does not exclude the value of academic disciplines but, while they are still necessary, they are no longer sufficient. Transdisciplinarity—both as a style of working and as an institutional structure—provides platforms for opening up thinking, teaching and research that weave together the

> expected and the unexpected, and that interface where learning most deeply occurs. It gives room for manoeuvre, discovery and invention. It provides students with a chance to practise intellectual, social and communication skills that, rather than being ancillary to learning, are always part of the inherent demonstration of learning and its enactment in the world. Using a philosophical discourse, Gray's work offers an invitation to a collaborative and transformative project of knowledge formation in a new space of learning that is *transdisciplinarity*.

The following interview is taken from an interview in with Gray in Hong Kong in January 2019.

What is your relationship to transdisciplinarity?

My relationship to transdisciplinarity predates even my own undergraduate studies, when I was beginning to think about how to understand how the universe works. I've always been interested in the very large questions: about how and why the universe operates? Obviously, every discipline has a take on that, which would need to be explicated at greater length, but I ended up studying philosophy and thoroughly loved that experience. I continue with these studies even now, although philosophy, for me, is always interconnected with other disciplines such as urban studies, literature and the arts. I subsequently completed two Masters in very different subjects and then, when I was looking at PhD programmes while studying at Yale, I decided against applying to those programmes because, at the time, the disciplinary boundaries felt overly constraining.

Upon starting to teach in Switzerland, I had my first experience of running a transdisciplinary humanities programme as the Director of Humanities in an international secondary school. This led me back to complete a PhD at Emory University in Interdisciplinary Studies before entering my formal professional trajectory into the transdisciplinary world at the University of Washington, Bothell. There, I was in charge of starting from scratch a brand new first-year programme, the Discovery Core, that was interdisciplinary in nature, and so I had to lead the effort to build courses and start thinking about transdisciplinarity in a more formal way, not just because it suited my temperament and intellectual disposition. Finally, it was in 2015, having arrived at HKU in 2014 to take up the Directorship of the Common Core, when I started more extensively thinking about the *concept* of transdisciplinarity. I began to feel a bit constrained by the 'inter' of interdisciplinarity, because most people wanted to define that too quickly as a relationship between already established disciplines. It's a working, operative principle, and I think the 'trans' serves as an operator, a kind of shifter, between social systems and intellectual domains.

What does TD practice mean to you?

It means mainly experimenting with new forms of learning relationships, but we should not take the word 'relationship' to simply represent human to human. Given the crises we are all facing, we have to expand our vision. I'm currently working on a project with Rick Dolphijn of Utrecht University called the *More Than Human City* which includes scales from the nano- to the cosmic, ions to physical infrastructure, biomes and microbes. A city is an assemblage of the human and non-human. A project of this nature allows for different types of work with a wide range of students from across both campuses, as well as architects, artists and scientists as we all build different institutional points of contact and points of resonance. We've also had the good fortune to work with the Wellcome Trust on a project called *Contagious Cities* and questions of transdisciplinary research. I've recently completed a book called *Urban Arabesques* that explores philosophy in the city including politics, the emergence of 'cities within cities' in an urban imaginary, and strange movements of critical figures such as the Pink Panther in relationship to Hong Kong's Umbrella Movement, beribboned lobsters walking in the streets and the burning of ghost money for the ancestors in Hong Kong, a city known for its international financial service. It's definitely a transdisciplinary scholarly effort. It's a writing project, connected to many developmental projects in the Common Core at HKU and around the world, and it has also expanded my reading list quite a bit.

What is distinctive about TD as opposed to multidisciplinarity v interdisciplinarity, etc.?

From my perspective, when exploring transdisciplinarity you have to keep it in movement across many boundaries. All the boundaries of TD are always provisional, and that's exactly as it should be. A classroom, for example, is a provisional community, it comes and goes, like companies, partnerships, projects, so you want to make each instance as high quality as possible, say thank you and all the best, and very often those partners will look back at the experience as a way of opening an unpredictable but powerful future.

With Rick Dolphijn from the University of Utrecht, we have created a transdisciplinary undergraduate research exchange that emerged from an evening in HKU's Black Box Theatre that I hosted on inventing the transdisciplinary university. There were people from all over, and we had a jam session about what a transdisciplinary university might look like. Then we wanted to begin to concretise that with the Utrecht experiment. Out of this opportunity, many different things have emerged in the last few years, including creating a group of light-touch researchers we call Transdisciplinary Nomads and working with the Wellcome Trust with colleagues from biomedicine, museums and landscape architecture. The project explored contagious cities, involving art, science, and sociology, among other things, in Geneva, New York and Hong Kong. At one of our transdisciplinary research meetings, I reflected on how these moments are so interesting because they mark a certain point in the history of the emergence of a discourse. A 'discourse', as you know, is not just language, but a full series of practices, and so I was thrilled to be part of that. We will also have a follow-up meeting later in the Fall of 2019 to see what we have learned from this experiment in transdisciplinarity.

What criteria do you use to acknowledge TD as plausible?

Focusing on the question of criteria and measurement, I think transdisciplinarity has to be *situated* knowledge, and those scenarios are all different depending on the day, the time, who's there, where we are, what the weather's like, what the objective is. There is no 'general method' that will work in each situation and I think a number of disciplines are reconsidering the relationship between old terms such as 'particular' and 'universal', trying to imagine different knowledge formation and types of rationalities that are more transdisciplinary with different protocols at work.

I think another criterion is that you see what emerges from the work without knowing ahead of time what might appear. I'm much more interested in transdisciplinarity as a series of working methods rather than a bounded object of knowledge, which it can never be. I think any object of knowledge includes within itself the entire cosmos (although obviously multiple relays must be activated). It's not a new object of knowledge exactly, but it's a new way of relationship building, knowledge production and social formation production. It's something analogous to the Surrealists' experiments with what they called 'forced analogies' or the Situationists experiments with the *dérives* of psychogeography.

Discovery and invention, of course, don't have to be transdisciplinary in all cases, but it can also happen 'within' any chemistry or philosophy class. I would argue, though, that even these by now naturalised disciplines are always transdisciplinary in nature but this cannot become sufficiently visible until certain dimensions of history, globalisation, cross-cultural and cross-disciplinary elements are brought to the foreground these shifting multi-faceted relationships.

Finally, another criterion is what is actually created out of transdisciplinary interactions, especially as we face such deeply vexatious issues such as migration, urbanisation, inequities of opportunity and wealth or climate change.

What values do you associate values with TD, knowing it differs from other forms of knowledge?

Disciplines are powerful formations, they produce amazing new knowledge, and they're not going away soon, but universities and all their partners have to create platforms and pathways for new formations or an insularity of thinking will begin to constrain certain types of creativity.

Its form as active formation and its product as process so it gives us different ways of working, taking account of different levels of the real and of what we know and how to reposition what we know towards different ends. I don't think it's a stabilised object of knowledge, and I don't think it should or can be. The complexity of our problems requires radical new ways of thinking and practicing.

It's really a different way of thinking. I like the word 'mode', and I believe a disposition of experimentalism of crossovers of knowledge, risk-taking, ambiguity and a range of types of precision, combined with conceptual and imaginative expansiveness, differentiates TD as a style of knowledge formation. This, in daily life, is relayed to the reward systems of universities, which operate almost exclusively along disciplinary lines, so these structures also need to be considered. We've just created five new interdisciplinary degrees at HKU and there are many other examples around the world, so I am encouraged that such programmes are now beginning to more formally coexist with traditional departments.

Who do you consider is shaping our understanding of TD?

For me, individually, it's mostly French and German philosophers, all of whom are deeply familiar, of course, with a range of different sciences. I would start with Nietzsche and then Freud, moving on to perhaps Heidegger in terms of questions concerning technology and his interest in art, mathematics and logic. There is Jacques Derrida, following these predecessors, with his interest in the very formation of conceptuality in Western thought. I'm also deeply intrigued by the work of Deleuze, which, along with his partner in writing Félix Guattari, has changed the ways in which we think about the relations across broad swathes of knowledge. These, along with Michel Serres, are the masters at these ways of thinking across histories and disciplines. Bruno Latour has also contributed significantly through works such as *We Have Never Been Modern* and *Down to Earth*.

The connection, for me, is their interest in what might be called the 'relations of relations', and there's nothing outside of relations of relations. How do we mediate, relay and connect different types of knowledge? How do we create overlay maps of what we know? I think we have to talk about the *milieu* and the *trans-* as types of terminology that do not depend on ideas of 'essence' that are reductionist or atomistic. Transdisciplinarity is a *multiplier* of ways of teaching, learning and producing knowledge.

I would also add the word 'translation' as a key principle for transdisciplinarity to thrive. We are all translators across all sorts of different contexts: university, non-university, disciplines, types of students and all the hierarchies of university life. Much of our job is translating.

What are the hurdles?

The history of institutionality is hugely important, and the fact that many institutions such as HKU and the University of Technology Sydney (UTS) have been willing to make space for our enterprises is all to the good. I would encourage every university to create spaces like this. It's not going to threaten the old-standing power structures, but it lets us do our work of seed-planting and partner-building. For many universities, faculties and departments are really the sources of financial power and most decision-making. Most of my job as Director of the Common Core is about persuasion and creating platforms of different teaching methods, course types and projects to see what can emerge. There is a need to find ways of encouraging the collegiality and enhance the intellectual excitement that is present in all universities. Much of education trains us to be careful, but one of the necessities of transdisciplinarity is a willingness to take risks, just try out new things.

Another constraint on transdisciplinarity is the obsession with a certain type of measurement and on occasion a misunderstanding of the use of measurement.

Precision takes different forms in different contexts, all of which need to be respected, but all forms of learning cannot be quantified.

Another hurdle relates to the concept of shared plenitude, because none of us are experts in everything, and so we really need each other to achieve the outcomes that come from transdisciplinarity. I need my colleagues to read everything they're reading, do all the experiments that they are working on in the lab, so that I will have the advantage of that, because I don't have time or skill to do all of that work. In turn, I'll read that chapter of Deleuze's in *The Logic of Sense* and tell you all about it. Plenitude is collegial, so a hurdle involves any constraints on sharing knowledge.

One final hurdle I often reflect on is finitude itself. Those of us who are curious want to be beginning again all the time, and that's both exciting and frustrating because there's so much we want to know and there's so little time. I think finitude is a definite, and definitive, hurdle for each of us individually, so we need to pass along as best we can as much as we can.

References

Kochhar-Lindgren, G. (2017a) Configuring interdisciplinarity: The common core at the University of Hong Kong. In L. S. Watts & P. Blessinger (Eds.), *Creative learning in higher education: International perspectives and approaches* (pp. 53–65). New York: Routledge.

Kochhar-Lindgren, G. (2017b). Trans-rational cash: Ghost-money, Hong Kong, and nonmodern networks. *Culture, Theory and Critique, 58*(1), 94–106.

Kochhar-Lindgren, G. (2017c). Hong Kong's liberal arts laboratory: Design-thinking, practical wisdom, and the common Core@HKU. In D. Araya & P. Marber (Eds.), *The evolution of the liberal arts in a global age* (pp. 173–183). Marber. New York: Routledge.

Kochhar-Lindgren, G. (2019). Scintillant@the University of Angelic Invention. In R. Dolphijn (Ed.), *Michel Serres and the crises of the contemporary* (pp. 106–126). London: Bloomsbury.

Kochhar-Lindgren, G., & Kochhar-Lindgren, K. (2018). Wild studios: Art, philosophy, and the transversal university. In D. R. Cole & J. P. N. Bradley (Eds.), *Principles of transversality in globalization and education* (pp. 31–46). Singapore: Springer.

Chapter 6
Kate Maguire

Kate Maguire is an Associate Professor in the Faculty of Professional and Social Sciences at Middlesex University, London, and Director of its transdisciplinary doctoral programmes. Her background is in social anthropology of the Middle East, trauma psychotherapy and authority dynamics. Since coming into higher education, she has engaged in developing innovative research pedagogies and methodologies relevant to professional practice. She has delivered papers on transdisciplinarity, aligning it to anthropology and examining its relevance to the contemporary pursuit of answers to complex micro and macro problems. She was drawn to professional practice research for the same reasons she remains informed by anthropology: to focus on the interconnectedness of knowledges rather than their separation. Co-generated knowledge has a role in creating the conditions for a more equitable share in decision-making processes to improve the societies in which we live.

Maguire's most significant writing on the subject might be *Transdisciplinarity as translation* (2015).

Transdisciplinarity as a Global Anthropology of Learning (2017) *and Transdisciplinarity: Towards an Epistemology of What Matters* (2018).

We regard Kate's position on transdisciplinarity captured in this short summary.

> The core elements of transdisciplinarity: real-world problem-solving; change agency; knowledge production; new synthesis; exchange between disciplines and practices with the intention of achieving action that influences the disciplines and practices themselves; mapping and remapping; academic and non-academic participation and social responsibility can lead to what can be called *metanoia*, another way of knowing; a knowing 'beyond' which is creative and transformative. This poses challenges for transdisciplinary approaches at doctoral level about the skills and attributes required of those who have the task of facilitating and negotiating this understanding between different realms of experience, thinking and cultures so that a *metanoia* can take place that supports the arriving at a change or response that is of benefit to the largest number of stakeholders. This involves not only the role of academics but the roles of the public

> in various forms such as the workplace senior practitioner; the spokesperson for a public health charity; the CEO of a major energy company; the people in a location where major change is being researched which will affect their lives and livelihoods; governments and international institutions tasked with protecting human rights and global sustainability through policies, guidelines and regulations.

The following are based upon an interview held with Kate in June 2018 when she was in England.

Can you offer a brief description of your intellectual relationship to transdisciplinarity? I know that you're a trained anthropologist, and that you've had issues, some things you've written have included that dimension.

I think anthropology is a great influence on how I have attached, if you like, to transdisciplinarity because it's not new for me, it resonates very much. But it takes on a form which is more sophisticated, and I think more relevant for the modern world, although anthropology is now catching up with these ideas. I studied psychology and anthropology at university but then it was the end of the '60s and you did anything that had an 'ology' at the end of it. So, I thought, well, psychology that's good, that'll help me understand things and understand myself better of course, and anthropology because it was just so exotic. But within a year of being at university, I felt with psychology, which was the behavioural school, that nothing resonated with my lived experience, but anthropology seemed to speak to me but I wasn't quite sure then of the why and the how of that. It was more than an intellectual engagement. It was quite a strong ontological engagement. I can't say the resonance was to do with coming from a multi-cultural society, for example. It wasn't that, quite the contrary. But there was something about attitudes to peoples, attitudes to difference. Maybe it was something to do with my parents. Both had served in the Second World War, but after the war, watching them, my mother throwing coins out of our Glasgow tenement window to Italian soldiers who had been wounded, and my father who was a policeman helping lots of people in the community, including refugees from everywhere after the war although we were poor ourselves. And in just watching them, I experienced in them a value towards how we are in the world, not 'how we do', but that the 'how we are' *informs* what we do. I am aware I'm looking back, and I might be making sense out of something that wasn't really there. But for me it was about that resonance. So, I have an intellectual appreciation for transdisciplinarity but a stronger ontological relationship with it.

But not necessarily with transdisciplinarity can you make those links?

Yes, because I think anthropology for me was the first step. I've had fantasies about all students needing to take a course in anthropology when they go to university because, first of all, it surfaces difference in a way which is non-judgmental. It's curious, it has a curiosity. I was curious, it helped me to see that actually I had deep curiosity about things, and it took that curiosity in quite a logical direction. If you're curious then how do you manifest your curiosity in a very positive way that would contribute to your own knowledge and inform your actions or positions. Transdisciplinarity was also giving me a conceptual framework built originally on anthropology and making it more sophisticated, because, in the meantime, the difference between the '70s and now is this incredible interconnectedness of things. Transdisciplinarity could offer something more relevant to faster moving contexts. What the anthropologists couldn't do to the extent we can now is to take these different studies and put them together and say something meaningful about the human condition in the interconnectedness of things, and that's what transdisciplinary notions began to address and in a very exciting way.

Transdisciplinary knowledge is in flux which fits so well into complexity, in notions of complexity and interconnectedness not being about pinning things down, it is about constant movement, and that constant movement is in itself a knowledge, it's a constant emergent knowledge, and its beauty is in evading the stagnant stasis of sacredness. We need disciplines, I think we need people who dig deep and are quite detailed, obsessive even and boundaried and I see transdisciplinarity more as working the way seafarers did, cross-pollinating, connecting things up and almost seeing what happens and, in a positive framing, facilitating understanding between these different hubs. Transdisciplinarity is generative in the in between.

Why does this take us to transdisciplinary practice? What does that mean to you?

Well I think that's something I've grappled with a lot in that I would have to put it in a context, first of all, of higher education, and my own position is that there is knowledge outside of the academy and there's knowledge within the academy, and they're not necessarily the same thing. I think there is a welcome trend in trying to build an interconnection between those two different realms of difference so that we do not silence or revere one kind of knowledge above the other but expand knowledge for both. That was the first step. I came into academics from long experience in professional and NGO sectors, I came in with a practitioner's knowledge which was rich and diverse to see what the academy had to offer that could illuminate me further, and how I might be able to, and this was at first challenging, illuminate the practices of the university in some small way. It was important to find a department to which I could belong and which wasn't rigidly single disciplined. I found one with an existing doctoral programme whose whole purpose was to do bridge that difference but in my opinion we didn't have a particularly strong theoretical underpinning in addition to that of work-based learning but the programme had taken progressive steps in widening methodological choices. In my opinion there was a gap, people were relying on methodologies rather than theories to try to see how we could interconnect these two realms of knowledge. Transdisciplinarity then began to offer something about how we can organise our thinking around those notions of interconnection and make sense to people who work in external organisations, external to the university, who in their senior roles are never really single disciplined. In a global world of trade and exchange, of cultural integration and complexity, an engineer running an engineering company is going to require some knowledge of a variety of different sectors in order to be successful at what they do and the types of people they manage. And these were the kinds of professionals that were attracted to the programme. I'm not saying they use the term transdisciplinary in their organisations, nor to describe what they do but once we spoke to them in those terms, it seemed to legitimise for them what they do in academic terms. This then opened up a whole new world of discourse for them that they wouldn't normally have been able to access and then find, unexpectedly, and I think this is one of the great things I've found on the programme, that these professionals later write and talk about experiencing a change that happens within them, that they can now access other discourses, that they're not confined to discipline or sector boundaries of discourse such as health, or education or engineering but they can borrow, or can use ideas and concepts beyond sector boundaries to illuminate and articulate the complexities of their professional situations, their work world cultures. For me, transdisciplinarity supplied us with a frame, an organising frame which starts with a conceptualisation of complex practice, and then from that conceptualisation arises two major things, one is understanding the interconnectedness of your own practices and how they shape and are shaped by contact with others, both within their own organisation or department or team and those external to themselves because now they can articulate the complexities of their practices to others which until that time have been implicitly known and not always explicitly expressed well. I think that's fundamentally important but so is the realisation that interconnection of knowledges, no matter how far apart you thought these knowledges were, in fact, is not as alien as you thought they would be, that they make sense in your world too, but you would never have known that before embarking on a programme that opens the doors rather than closes them. In that way, transdisciplinarity works, not just in infusing knowledge with difference but it works on your own knowledge, it helps you to formulate, reformulate and grow your own understanding in the world in which you live and the practices which you do, but you're informed now about the practices and are open to reshaping them.

What do you think, from your practice, from your experience, from the way in which you engage with people, is distinctive about the creation of transdisciplinary knowledge?

It's a good question, it's probably the one that occupies me the most because we don't really do evaluation studies on this. But there is something about, the 'trans' part of transdisciplinarity, Nicolescu talks about going between and beyond disciplines. And I think that, certainly on the programme that we have here, the beyond is for me, the most interesting concept because yes, I did talk about the practice and the combination, but what emerges from the combination? It's a shift in ontology, it's a shift in how you look at the world and look at your place in the world, and so, for example, you might have somebody who comes into the programme wanting to do research into their practice, and through the discourses a number of dimensions of their practice surface. For example, they increase their explicit understanding of what they do and why and what informs their choices and particularly the impact their choices and what they value, what matters to them, have on others and the responses of others. And then at the end of the day, through that close observation of their practice, through notions of reflection and reflexivity in situations of complexity, something fundamentally shifts in their approach, their attitude to being in the world which informs what they do differently and how they respond to what others have to say and offer. In many ways, they're not just 'doing' now, they have an attitude of 'being', how they look at something, how they look at difference, how they look at engagement, how they look at diversity, how they look at collaboration and working with and in teams, how they look at authority. Someone was saying something about TD perhaps having too much of a moral compass, but I like the idea of TD having a moral compass because we have very serious problems in the world being addressed by TD approaches as nothing else seems to work effectively. TD is not only an approach to individual or team practice but also an approach to resolving the big problems, Timothy Morton's notion of how we communicate with the hyperobjects, those which are so large and amorphous like climate change which require us to put aside assumptions, perceptions, knowledge territories, vested financial interests and ideologies in order to come to the table and work together on what matters to our very survival. Just the very inclusion of people whom we never included before, the so-called non-experts, but whose lives will be more severely affected than those with invested commercial interests at a distance, to me is, even if it's a by-product, a moral statement in the world. At the other end of that spectrum TD helps us to come to the table and resolve what matters in a team, what matters in an organisation to the people who run it at all levels and to the communities in which it sits. I think, something about the distinctiveness of TD is not just about the product of some kind at the end, it's the process of arriving at something. It requires a suspension of, or a putting in the background, your own disciplinary training, and your own assumptions, and opening up and listening. I'm very struck by the relational principles of Carl Rogers one of which is congruence, and others include being non-judgmental and having positive regard. Congruence is the most challenging, being the same person internally and externally. Or as Stan Lester puts it, the difference between being *a* professional and being professional That's a good enough beginning for an ethical stance. If you're looking at climate change and you include in the littoral parts of the world, the fisherman, the people that have their little cafes along a shore road and you have the climatologists and you have the big gun experts, and you include them all at a table and say, OK, let's have a look at this, instead of, and this is probably quite idealistic on my part, but instead of the climatologist saying, this is how we do it, and an architect saying, this is how we need to protect the corporate buildings what if everyone just listened to each other with the Rogerian principles and were in touch with their own cognitive dissonance; what, instead of your paradigm talking for you, you speak for yourself as well? This provides the conditions for the co-creation of new knowledge and 'co' is key here. Yes the ontology comes into the space, that's my fantasy if you like about it. I have more faith in that bringing about change than intellectualising about it.

What are the conditions or environments that are needed for transdisciplinary activities or attitude, whichever phrase you think's most appropriate to flourish and thrive, or the inverse, what are the barriers?

Well I think, again, one of the things which has emerged out of these last few years is how much we are obstacles to our own knowledge, that we are the barriers, and I think that that's the case in a university environment. That we can be territorial and entrenched; there seems to be some fear and when there is fear you can rubbish other territories, and be suspicious of things that are not in the traditional sense reliable; anything that even hints at subjectivity, for example. I think there's lots of misunderstandings. I think there's more understanding of transdisciplinary practices outside the university than there is within the university. I would say what would help higher education to flourish in this new world is an open-mindedness, not trying to manage uncertainty or mitigate uncertainties but to go with them and see uncertainties as opportunities. I would think that the university could do, well any university can do well to be more open, to not just focus on the exchange they're trying to do with the outside, but look at what exchange they can do, knowledge exchange and sharing that they can do within the university to really look at what paradigms they are using, what criteria that they are using when we're looking at the value of research, to be more creative about how people do research, how they present research, how they assess research, strong impacts on how one arrives at a contribution to the world. So yes, I think it's been difficult to find a place for transdisciplinary approaches but I'm quite optimistic that people who do come in contact with it, or come in contact even with multidisciplinary thinking, are seeing that it actually reflects the world that we live in much more. It's as if universities are in danger of remaining islands, people in that work world could go out of more and with more openness to being changed by the experience because otherwise it's creating a distance between what we all know in reality is out there but not responding appropriately with the great knowledge resources the university has at its disposal to share. For the moment, Paul, we enjoy transdisciplinarity's role in providing at least some conditions for changes in attitudes and perspective to take place.

References

Maguire, K. (2015). Transdisciplinarity as translation. In P. Gibbs (Ed.), *Transdisciplinary professional learning and practice* (pp. 165–177). Switzerland: Springer International Publishing.

Maguire, K. (2017). Transdisciplinarity as a global anthropology of learning. In *Transdisciplinary higher education—A theoretical basis revealed in practice* (pp. 163–176). Cham: Springer International Publishing AG.

Maguire, K. (2018). Transdisciplinarity: Towards an epistemology of what matters. In D. Fam, L. Neuhauser & P. Gibbs (Eds.), *Transdisciplinary theory, practice and education: The art of collaborative research and collective learning* (pp. 103–116).

Chapter 7
Julie Thompson Klein

Julie Thompson Klein is Professor of Humanities Emerita at Wayne State University in Detroit, Michigan (USA) and International Research Affiliate in the Transdisciplinary Lab at ETH-Zurich (Switzerland). Holder of a Ph.D. in English from the University of Oregon, she is past president of the Association for Integrative Studies (AIS) and former editor of the AIS journal, *Issues in Integrative Studies*. She is a prolific author and thought leader, having authored and co/edited numerous books and monographs on interdisciplinarity including *The Oxford Handbook of Interdisciplinarity*. She consults widely throughout North America and the world. She has served as a Fulbright Lecturer and an Academic Specialist in Nepal, a Visiting Foreign Professor in Japan and a Foundation Visitor in New Zealand. She also created the Digital Humanities Collaboratory at Wayne State and serves on the Steering Committee of the Humanities, Arts, Science, and Technology Advanced Collaboratory (HASTAC). In 2017, she was the Distinguished Woman in Residence at the University of British Columbia, showcasing her work on interdisciplinarity and digital humanities, and also in that year received the Science of Team Science Recognition Award. In addition, she is a member of the board of directors of the International Network for the Science of Team Science (INSciTS) and a founding member of the international ITD Alliance. She is currently working on a new book entitled 'Beyond interdisciplinarity: Boundary work, communication, and collaboration in the twenty-first century'.

This short summary presents Julie's position on inter- and transdisciplinarity:

> Julie's most recent work explores boundary work, which she argues includes the plurality and complexity of crossing boundaries of academic disciplines, interdisciplinary fields and sectors of society including government, industry and the public sphere. She also tracks trajectories, methodologies, theoretical positions, schools of thought and institutional locations of inter- and transdisciplinary fields, examining dynamics of integration and collaboration in trading zones of expertise and communities of practice.
>
> Julie also advocates for strategies that move beyond narrow skills training to help students navigate their futures by understanding the complexity of the world they live

> in, coping with change by learning how to learn, steering between extremes and cultivating a new literacy grounded in skills of deep and critical thinking and integration, communication and collaboration, and cross-cultural understanding. Having a 'palpable impact' does not mean jettisoning everything but keeping what works well while shedding inherited features by 'unbundling' and 'rebundling' practices.

The following interview is taken from a conversation with Julie in April 2019.

What does TD practice mean to you?

Transdisciplinarity (TD) is part of a family of terms for boundary crossing. My own engagement with TD stems from decades of research on the history, theory and practice of interdisciplinarity. Given a background in humanities, my methodology triangulates rhetorical, historical and sociological analysis. Rhetorical analysis examines claims by which people construct a field or a concept, consensus and difference, and ways keywords structure hierarchies of value. Historiographical analysis uncovers genealogies of origin, periodisations, continuity and change. Sociological analysis, in turn, is a vital partner to humanities because it examines how individuals and groups establish identity, authority and reputational systems. Understanding transdisciplinarity, then, requires identifying patterns of definition, shifts over time and communities of practice that adopt particular meanings.

Linguists attribute shifts in meaning to multiple causes, though four processes stand out (Ullman, 1962). The first cause—*Pejoration*—signals negative connotations, evident in critiques of transdisciplinarity's historical alignment with unity of knowledge and more recent prioritising of problem-solving over philosophy. The second—*Amelioration*—is linked with the latter development, in widespread favouring of problem-solving as the raison d'etre of TD. The third—*Narrowing*—marks restricted or specialised uses, evident in contests over the 'true' meaning of transdisciplinarity. And, the fourth—*Broadening*—acknowledges expansion of meaning since conventional dating of the term's origin to 1970, in a typology of definitions created for the first international conference on interdisciplinary research and teaching (Klein, forthcoming).

Philosopher McKeon (1971) once observed that all terminology embodies principles of both continuity and discontinuity, and even continuing terms assume new meanings in new applications. Transdisciplinarity is no exception. As a result, Frodeman (2017) contended when introducing the latest edition of *The Oxford Handbook of Interdisciplinarity*, inter- and transdisciplinarity are both boundary objects with different meanings at different times for different groups.

What is distinctive about the creation of TD knowledge in relation to disciplinary, multi, inter?

In a book of case studies on interdisciplines Graff (2015) faulted the 'name game' of terminology for generating more confusion than clarity, charging 'The endless typologies, classifications, and hierarchies of multi-, inter-, and transdisciplinarities are not helpful'. However, clear patterns of consensus counter are evident, tracked in my chapters for the 2010 and 2017 editions of *The Oxford Handbook of Interdisciplinarity*. A literature review and workshop on definition sponsored by the INTREPID network of researchers, practitioners and policymakers from 27 countries shed further light on the matter. Keywords of 'cooperation', 'trust' and 'integration' appeared across multi-, inter- and transdisciplinarity. Interdisciplinarity, though, was linked primarily with connectedness and combination, while TD was associated with normative dimensions and change. Even so, Von Wehrden et al. (2018), cautioned, any general definition is complicated by involvement of actors outside the academy.

This book's editors join others in dating the term 'transdisciplinarity' to the typology introduced in 1970. The definition was a common system of axioms that transcends the narrow scope of disciplinary worldviews through an overarching synthesis, exemplified by anthropology as an overarching science of humans. It accentuated a higher level of synthesis than 'interdisciplinary' combinations of existing disciplinary approaches. Three participants in the conference, though, differed on specifics. Jean Piaget treated TD as an aspirational stage in the epistemology of interdisciplinary relationships based on reciprocal assimilations. Andre Lichnerowicz promoted 'the mathematic' as a universal interlanguage, and in further contrast, Erich Jantsch imbued TD with social purpose in a hierarchical model of the system of science, education and innovation in Apostel et al. (1972).

Since then, the term has proliferated. It now appears as a label for a variety of overarching frameworks, synoptic disciplines such as anthropology and philosophy, a team-based holistic approach to health care, a comprehensive student-centred curriculum, and trans-sector co-production of knowledge with academics and stakeholders. In each case, the original Latin meaning of the adjective 'trans' movement through and beyond something is apparent. However, differences appear, linked with discourses of philosophy and problem-solving.

What are the criteria you use to acknowledge TD as plausible knowledge, can you relate notions of epistemology, ontology and metaphysics to how you understand TD knowledge or do these terms not fit TD reality?

Plausibility assumes that something is reasonable and credible, verified by meeting criteria a group holds in common. Shared beliefs about reality shaped initial philosophical discourse of interdisciplinarity, traced in the West from ancient Greece forward to the idea of unity. This idea persisted in a variety of initiatives ranging from the medieval Christian summa and Enlightenment ambition of universal reason to Umberto Eco's speculation on a perfect language and Transcendentalism to the Unity of Science movement and search for unification theory in physics to E. O. Wilson's theory of consilience and curricula that continue to cultivate the 'whole person'. Reviewing the history of transdisciplinarity, philosopher Kockelmans (1979) concluded it has tended to centre on educational and philosophical dimensions of sciences. However, he argued, the search for unity today does not follow automatically from a pre-given, presupposed order of things. It must be continually 'brought about' through critical, philosophical and supra-scientific reflection.

Examples range widely in focus, from a general ethos or attitude to new paradigms anchored in particular fields. Basarab Nicolescu illustrates the former in this book, in a major initiative to foster a new universality of thought and type of education advanced by the International Center for Transdisciplinary Research. This effort, which I first encountered at the First World Congress of Transdisciplinarity, held in 1994 at the Convento de Arrábida of Portugal, replaces reductionism with a principle of relativity informed by the new worldview of complexity in science. Its scope is broad, spanning transcultural, transnational, ethical, spiritual and creative dimensions (http://perso.club-internet.fr/nicol/ciret). The emergence of new paradigms also labelled 'transdisciplinary' documents the latter kind of example, pluralising meaning in subject-specific areas as varied as general systems theory, Marxism, feminist theory, post/structuralism and sustainability.

The work of a fellow member in the US-based Association for Interdisciplinary Studies, which was my initial professional home for cross-disciplinary research and education in the 1980s, illuminates the attendant variety. All conceptual frameworks associated with the term 'transdisciplinarity', Miller (1982) explained, claim to transcend the narrow scope of disciplinary worldviews and metaphorically encompass parts of a material field disciplines handle separately. However, they do not all converge naturally because their languages and worldviews differ. Some proponents also believe their frameworks should replace existing disciplinary approaches, while others consider them alternatives or sources of coherence for cross-disciplinary efforts. They claim different types of isomorphism, as well, between their conceptual structures and the 'real world' they purportedly represent. They exhibit differing receptivity to quantitative and empirical methods. And, some emanated from socio-political movements outside the academy, including Marxism and feminist theory.

Do you associate values with TD knowing in ways that differ from the other forms of knowledge?

Values, like plausibility, are contingent upon context. Pragmatic values in the discourse of problem-solving became so influential that they fostered a broad shift from the earlier prominence of epistemology in conceptions of transdisciplinarity. Work in environmental research during the late 1980s and early 1990s in German and Swiss contexts signalled a historical expansion of meaning. The core premise is that problems of the *Lebenswelt*—the lifeworld—need to frame research questions and practices, not disciplines. By 2000, at the first major international conference on transdisciplinarity and joint problem-solving, case studies were reported in all fields of human interaction with natural systems and technical innovations as well as the development context (Klein et al. 2001). Jahn, Bergmann and Keil called the benchmark meeting a 'normative turn' in prioritising real-world problems (2012, p. 2).

Given the location of that conference in Switzerland, it has been dubbed the 'Zurich approach'. Yet, parallel developments in Germany and Austria were also central to redefinition. Serving on the planning board for the conference in Zurich introduced me to aligned developments in German-speaking countries of Europe as well as an emerging global movement. Over 800 people from 51 countries attended that conference, representing European initiatives as well as North–South partnerships. Subsequently, TD gained a wider footprint in international conferences of the

Network for Transdisciplinary Research (td-net), which have acquainted me with parallel work in Latin America, Australia and Africa. In each case shared commitments to solving societal problems and including stakeholders are apparent while also being responsive to local contexts. The same caveat holds when Nicolescu's initiative is characterised as the 'French school' of TD since it is an international network. Yet, the concept of pluridisciplinarité was more prominent in a recent seminar in Paris at L'Ecole des Hautes Etudes en Sciences Sociales. Similarly, there is no 'Anglo School' across English-speaking countries, though in the United States one definition has attained the status of a major exemplar.

In 2006, the US-based National Cancer Institute hosted a conference on team science that aligned transdisciplinarity with new conceptual and methodological frameworks for health and wellness. Kessel and Rosenfield (2008) called the meeting a 'turning point' in understanding the need for transdisciplinary research in health. Framed as 'transcendent interdisciplinary research', it is central to 'team science' and 'transdisciplinary science' in broad areas such as cancer research. Participation in the 2006 meeting and election to the board of directors for the International Network for the Science of Team Science have deepened my understanding of this sector even as I work with others to broaden its focus to include sustainability. Service on the US-based National Research Council's task force on Convergence further exposed me to trans-sector bridging of academic disciplines, industry, government and occupational professions that Sharp and Langer (2001) styled as the third of three revolutions. The first was molecular and cellular biology, and the second, genomics. Framed as a 'higher level of synthesis' and an 'expanded form of interdisciplinarity', Convergence is aligned with TD to highlight intersections of life/medicine/physical/and computational sciences as well as engineering. Outcomes include inventions in biodesign, energy storage, tissue engineering, optics in telecommunications, advances in neuroscience and new treatment protocols for disease (Committee, 2014).

All the while, the discourse of Critique continues to be a multi-layered interrogation of the existing structure of knowledge and education, the system of disciplinarity, and 'instrumental', 'strategic', 'pragmatic' or 'opportunistic' forms that prioritise the marketplace and national needs over questions of value and purpose. Together they move beyond, even while encompassing, the rhetoric of transcending boundaries to transgressing them. This vision of TD is especially prominent in humanities and interdisciplinary fields that emerged from movements external to the academy, including Black, women's and ethnic studies. In the 1990s, 'transdisciplinarity' also began appearing in humanities as a label for knowledge formations associated with new theoretical approaches and initiatives that rejected historical values of wholeness. Moreover, Vickers (1997) reported, TD became aligned with movements that raised questions of social and political justice silent in instrumental problem-solving while incorporating transdisciplinary theories of knowledge and culture outside the academy, including indigenous knowledge and lay expertise.

Who do you consider is shaping our understanding of TD?

Asking who is shaping 'our' understanding of TD begs the question of who 'we' are. Like interdisciplinarity, transdisciplinarity is a conflicted discourse. Rhetorics of 'holism' and 'synthesis' compete with 'problem-solving' and 'innovation' as well as 'transgression' and 'critique'. However, as authors of the 3rd INTREPID report put it, 'diversity does not have to be an adversity' (Von Wehrden et al. 2017). Differences matter. Communities of practice have their own bodies of literature and core groups, with selective references to influential authors in other enclaves. Yet, broad trends are also apparent. The primary organising languages of the 1970 conference were logic, cybernetics, general systems theory, structuralism and organisation theory. Systems theory continues to be the most widely influential, though complexity now looms large in the rhetorics of both inter- and transdisciplinarity. The heightened priority of problem-solving has also led to shared concepts across discourses of philosophy, problem-solving and critique, including 'postnormal science', 'wicked problems' and 'Mode 2 knowledge production'.

The first two concepts are closely associated with TD because both eschew reductionist and mechanistic assumptions, while recognising that a high divergence of values and factual knowledge shape theory and practice. Gibbons et al.'s (1994) theory of Mode 2 knowledge production also aligned TD with complexity, nonlinearity and heterogeneity while asserting a new social distribution of knowledge is occurring as a wider range of organisations and stakeholders contribute skills and expertise to problem-solving. Gibbons, et al. initially highlighted instrumental contexts of application, such as aircraft design, pharmaceutics and electronics. Subsequently, though, Nowotny, Scott and Gibbons (2001) extended Mode 2 theory to argue that contextualisation of problems requires participation in the *agora* of public debate, incorporating the discourse of democracy. When lay perspective and alternative knowledges are recognised, a shift occurs from solely reliable scientific knowledge to 'socially robust knowledge'. Drawing on the track record of sustainability, a field that embodies both problem-solving and critique, Scholz et al. (2011) further argued that socially robust knowledge addressing real-world challenges involves a form of epistemic that bridges scientific and experiential knowledge.

New forms of professional practice also bridge discourses. Introducing a book on TD in architecture and urban planning, Doucet and Janssens (2011) contended the gap between critical theories and projective design is being bridged as their relationship is situated in particular contexts, responsive to stakeholders, and open to change. Whether refitting metropolitan areas because of growth or moving cities because of climate change, questions of design are not separate from social, political and normative concerns. Ethics are also placed inside disciplinary and professional work rather than a peripheral afterthought. New objects come into view, new configurations of practices emerge and once excluded forms of knowledge are incorporated including the experience of laypeople. Fry (2011) described transdisciplinarity in the book as a form of *relational thinking* that not only dissolves disciplinary differences. It constitutes a conceptual leap in a form of 'redirective practice' that creates new ways of dealing with complexity. 'Problems are never received', Fry asserted, 'but always interrogated and redefined'.

What are the hurdles that challenge transdisciplinary ways of thinking?

Reports from science-policy bodies, educational commissions and professional organisations, as well as a growing body of case studies, have delineated barriers and disincentives. Despite agreement on factors for success, however, projects, programmes and even fields continue to falter. Comparison of benchmark reports and studies reveals common obstacles in all aspects of organisational structure and administration, procedures and policies, funding, resources and infrastructure, recognition and reward. Differences in modes of work and forms of knowledge are also compounding factors in trans-sector work. Resources abound as well. However, Bozeman and Boardman (2013) cautioned, even 'best practices' may not work across contexts and circumstances.

Nonetheless, a number of overarching principles have emerged from theory and practice of across-disciplinary work:

(1) transparency in all aspects of boundary work, including integration and collaboration;
(2) informed use of best practices, guidelines and models;
(3) consistency and alignment of separate activities in a systematic approach;
(4) appropriate criteria and a multi-methodological approach to evaluation;
(5) negotiation of differing interests in multi-institutional and cross-sectoral work and
(6) credit for rather than marginalisation or dismissal of cross-boundary outcomes.

Awareness of strategies and mechanisms is key to action. A number of *repositories* are excellent places to begin, to insure both theory and practice are informed and networked. I would particularly highlight three:

This *I2S* website is part of a global initiative to improve research on complex real-world problems. The 'Resources' link presents tools, cases and approaches along with information about pertinent journals, professional association and networks, and conferences (*Integration and Implementation Sciences*): i2s.anu.edu.au.

Td-net has an online toolbox called 'Co-producing Knowledge' that focuses on solving complex problems in collaboration with stakeholders. It provides links to methods, practical experiences, criteria and other related toolboxes. Related bibliography also includes works the network has published (*Network for Transdisciplinary Research, known as* http://www.transdisciplinarity.ch/).

The US-based National Cancer Institute's Team Science Toolkit is a user-generated searchable repository of resources on methods and measures along with an annotated bibliography. It includes online resource links to 'TeamScience.net' with learning modules (http://www.teamsciencetoolkit.cancer.gov/public/home.aspx).

A final question arises. Who is responsible for easing hurdles? The answer is all parties. Benchmark reports target actions for individuals and teams, universities, professional associations, funding agencies, government, industry and communities.

However, all parties are responsible for informed approaches in a systematic rather than a piece-meal manner. They are all responsible for transparency throughout the life cycles of projects, programmes and fields. And, they are responsible for matching rhetoric of endorsement with proactive support in the reward structure.

References

*Note: Responses to interview questions drew in large part on material in a forthcoming book, "Beyond interdisciplinarity: Boundary work, communication, and collaboration in the 21st century".

Apostel, L., et al. (Eds.). (1972). *Interdisciplinarity, problems of teaching and research in universities*. OECD, Paris. Jantsch, E. "Towards interdisciplinarity and transdisciplinarity in education and innovation," 97–121; Lichnerowicz, A. "Mathematic and transdisciplinarity", 121–127; Piaget, J. "The epistemology of interdisciplinary relationships", 127–139.

Bozeman, B., & Boardman, C. (2013). *An evidence-based assessment of research collaboration and team science: Patterns in industry and university-industry partnerships*. Presented at National Research Council Workshop on Institutional and Organizational Supports for Team Science, 24 October 2013, Washington, DC. Retrieved May, 2015, from http://sites.nationalacademies.org/DBASSE/BBCCSS/DBASSE_085236.

Committee on Convergence. National Research Council of the National Academies. (2014). *Convergence: Transdisciplinary integration of life sciences, physical sciences, engineering, and beyond*. Washington, DC: The National Academies Press.

Doucet, I., & Janssens, N. (2011). Editorial, transdisciplinarity the hybridization of knowledge production and space-related research. In I. Doucet & N. Janssens (Eds.), *Transdisciplinary knowledge production in architecture and urbanism towards hybrid modes of inquiry* (pp. 1–14). Dordrecht: Springer.

Frodeman, R. (2017). The future of interdisciplinarity: An introduction to the 2nd edition. In R. Frodeman, J. T. Klein, & R. Pacheco (Eds.), *The Oxford handbook of interdisciplinarity* (pp. 3–8). Oxford: Oxford University Press.

Fry, T. (2011). Getting over architecture: Thinking, surmounting, and redirecting. In I. Doucet & N. Janssens (Eds.), *Transdisciplinary knowledge production in architecture and urbanism towards hybrid modes of inquiry* (pp. 24–27). Dordrecht: Springer.

Gibbons, M., et al. (1994). *The new production of knowledge*. Newbury Park, CA and London: Sage.

Graff, H. J. (2015). *Undisciplining knowledge: Interdisciplinarity in the twentieth century*. Baltimore, MD: Johns Hopkins University Press.

Jahn, R., Bergmann, M., & Keil, F. (2012). Transdisciplinarity: Between mainstreaming and marginalization. *Ecological Economics, 79*, 1–10.

Kessel, F., & Rosenfield, P. (2008). Toward transdisciplinary research historical and contemporary perspectives. *American Journal of Preventive Medicine, 35*(2S), S225–S234.

Klein, J. T. (forthcoming). Beyond interdisciplinarity: Changing scale and space. In *Book from conference on Politiques et pratiques de L'nterdisciplinarité*, Paris.

Klein, J. T., Grossenbacher-Mansuy, W., Häberli, R., Bill, A., Scholz, R. W., & Welti, M. (Eds.). (2001). *Transdisciplinarity: Joint problem solving among science, technology, and society*. Basel: Birkhäuser.

Kockelmans, J. (1979). Why interdisciplinarity? In J. Kockelmans (Ed.), *Interdisciplinarity and higher education* (pp. 123–160). University Park: Pennsylvania State University Press.

McKeon, R. (1971). The Uses of rhetoric in a technological age: Architectonic productive arts. In L. F. Bitzer, & E. Black (Eds.), *The prospect of rhetoric* (pp. 44–63). Englewood Cliffs, NJ: Prentice-Hall.

References

Miller, R. (1982). Varieties of interdisciplinary approaches in the social sciences. *Issues in Integrative Studies, 1,* 1–37.

Nowotny, H., Scott, P., & Gibbons, M. (2001). *Re-thinking science: Knowledge and the public in an age of uncertainty.* Cambridge: Polity Press.

Scholz, R. W., et al. (2011). *Environmental literacy in science and society.* Cambridge: Cambridge University Press.

Sharp, P. A., & Langer, R. (2011). Promoting convergence in biomedical science. *Science, 333*(6042), 527.

Ullman, S. (1962). *Semantics: An introduction to the science of meaning.* Oxford: Blackwell.

Vickers, J. (1997). [U]framed in open, unmapped fields: Teaching and the practice of interdisciplinarity. *Arachnè An Interdisciplinary Journal of the Humanities, 4*(2), 11–42.

Von Wehrden, et al. (2017). 3rd INTREPID Report: Interdisciplinary and transdisciplinary research: Finding the common ground of multi-faceted concepts. Retrieved from 3rd-INTREPID-Report-ID-TD-WG1-1.pdf.

Von Wehrden, et al. (2018). Interdisciplinary and transdisciplinary research: Finding the common ground of multi-faceted concepts. *Sustainability Science.* Retrieved from https://doi.org/10.1007/s11625-018-0594-x.

Chapter 8
Linda Neuhauser

Linda Neuhauser is Clinical Professor of Community Health Sciences at the School of Public Health, University of California, Berkeley (USA), and is Visiting Professor in the Department of Social and Population Sciences at Nanjing Youdian University (Nanjing, China). She is also Co-Principal Investigator of the Health Research for Action Center (HRA) at the UC Berkeley School of Public Health. Her teaching, research and practice are focused on using participatory methods across disciplines and societal sectors to engage diverse groups to identify and solve problems. She and her colleagues have used participatory and transdisciplinary methods to co-create, co-implement and co-evaluate health and social interventions in many countries. She has written extensively on transdisciplinarity and, of her works, those that we consider the most influential are: *Advancing Transdisciplinary and Translational Research Practice: Issues and models of doctoral education in public health* (2007); *Integrating Transdisciplinary and Translational Concepts and Methods into Graduate Education* (2014); *Transdisciplinary Theory, Practice and Education* (2018); Collaborative research and action: The China Worker Wellness Project (2018) and Practical and scientific foundations of transdisciplinary research and action (2018).

We regard Linda's position on transdisciplinarity to be captured in this short summary:

> The 'scientific revolution' that emerged in the mid-1900s transformed thinking about the nature of reality and ways of thinking about it. The current view is that, because reality is complex, contextual and dynamically changing, it should be studied from as many perspectives as possible using multiple theoretical frameworks, methods and settings. Further, the realisation that narrow disciplinary research conducted in controlled conditions has not been effective in addressing complex problems like climate change, poverty or global security has catalysed efforts to integrate and apply knowledge across disciplines and societal sectors. Such 'transdisciplinary' approaches that link diverse researchers, practitioners and policymakers are improving scientific inquiry and its application to benefit society.

The following text is based on an interview with Linda in June 2018, when she was in the United States.

Can you offer a brief description of your intellectual relationship to transdisciplinarity?

Well, I come at these issues from an interest in trying to deal with really complex problems, especially in the health arena. There we have not done very well with solving complicated health problems. In my view, transdisciplinarity (TD)—the whole theoretical and practical aspect of it is the best fit to connect science with practice. Before TD, we had a lot of different theoretical frameworks and so forth, and those have not really worked very well. They've been too fragmented, and so transdisciplinarity has really been the thing that could bring together all of the theoretical issues that are involved in looking at problems, and also in trying to address them, trying to solve them.

What does transdisciplinary practice mean to you? How does it differ from other practice?

The first thing I'll mention is that when I was getting interested in transdisciplinarity and beginning to work on it, it was an 'Aha' moment because, as I mentioned, I come at this whole issue from a practice standpoint, that is, my motivation is actually to do things, rather than to necessarily think about new theories. However, the more I've gotten into it, I've become a lot more interested in the theoretical aspect. So, what my perspective is that we can't really de-link transdisciplinary theory, research and practice. If we try to say, 'well this is more relevant to practice, and this is more relevant to TD theory', then it doesn't really work. That's the perspective that I operate from. And when we look at TD practice specifically, I think it means finding a common issue to address, drawing guidance from as many relevant disciplines as possible, and then engaging relevant stakeholders from sectors in society. It's very complicated to think about all of this together, to try to think about all the disciplines that might affect a common issue that we're trying to solve, and then who all the relevant stakeholders are in society. I have many examples of that.

One example is the China Worker Wellness Project. This is a project in Changzhou, China that uses a TD approach to support migrant workers—non-resident citizens who have come from rural areas to work in urban factory zones. There are over 250 million such workers in China and they experience serious health and social problems. Many prior government interventions with migrant factory workers in China were well-intentioned but narrowly focused on medical care (discipline of medicine), but were not effective in identifying and addressing the many complex problems facing the workers. The Chinese government asked our Health Research for Action Center to help them develop a more effective approach. We started an entirely new way to deal with the problem, which was to look at all of the determinants of health and wellness related to worker issues that led to an understanding that many different disciplines were involved in issues related to migrant workers' health, so that's obviously medicine and public health, and things like that, but also legal issues, housing issues, job training and so forth. So, you might have twenty disciplines that are really relevant to trying to address the workers' problems. And then we introduced the idea of to needing to work with many stakeholders; not just the government but also with service providers; with the workers themselves, because they had never really been asked about what the issues were from *their* point of view. Also, talking to managers in factories because they also have many important perspectives; talking to the media; talking to many, many different groups in society and bringing all of these stakeholders together—people from different disciplines, people from different sectors and using participatory processes to identify the issues and then to gradually come up with solutions to those problems. This project started about 6 years ago and we have been very successful in using the TD approach, whereas prior projects had not worked out. We started with two factories and the project is now in over 28 factories. In each new factory, the workers, managers and other stakeholders use the TD process to create their own unique perspectives of problems and their own specific solutions for them. It's been very complex, but it's also been very effective for the workers and for the factories, too, and for the health sector. That's just one example of our work using a TD approach.

Is TD know-how somehow different from other knowledges?

Yes, it really is, and obviously the process I just referred to is very different and involves of course, bringing together people from many disciplines and stakeholders from many sectors, including the people who are the end beneficiaries. And along the way of using this process, the idea is that the knowledge that's created out of it is going to be very different. It's going to be a lot richer because it draws on many, many different disciplines, and it also comes from the perspectives of people from many sectors in society and many different positions in society. That kind of knowledge is very rich in that sense, and it also can result in things that *transcend* our usual disciplinary knowledge. For example, looking at the project in China, originally the traditional approach was to look just at health disciplines like medicine, but when others were added in, it really became a lot more transcendent way to think about the problems from many perspectives. It became a way to think more about a holistic life perspective rather than just fragmenting health from the issues that a person might face in this very new situation of being a migrant factory worker. That transcendent knowledge is much richer and so, when you think from a methodological point of view, this can lead to developing new frameworks. In the China project, we developed new frameworks of ways to think about migrant workers' overall wellness. These were much more built-out frameworks in the sense that they included at a lot more issues in people's lives, and in terms of interventions, they explored a lot of different ways to approach those issues. Because of this, there were a lot more solutions generated and a lot more practical solutions that actually worked.

Also, this TD approach will generate new methods. We used a lot of methods in this project that are very different from a typical disciplinary project or a project that is investigator run. Those methods involve ways to, bring people together, and bring the different stakeholders together into groups. We use design science methods such as design thinking, and we customise each of these methods for the specific project itself. For example, in the China project, workers in each factory came up with unique ways to engage other workers in the project. Because we are working in 28 factories, that means there are 28 different methods for worker engagement. I think this is one hallmark of TD work: you take methods that exist already, but you can make a 'mash up'. You can put those methods together and then customise them, so they actually fit what you're trying to do.

Another example is using design thinking methods in the context of China. We know that design thinking methods that are very popular in Western society. These methods were created originally at Stanford University in California in the United States, and now they have spread around the world. But they have taken on something of a Western flavour, given how they were created, and we found that in China it was really necessary to work together with people to customise those methods so that they worked out much better in that cultural, governmental and industrial context. There's a lot of refinement that goes on with a TD project, and we don't often hear about these small refinements because people tend, in scientific work, they tend to just identify a generic method 'We used focus groups in our research', when in TD work they're actually doing something quite unique: they're making a new version of a method. That's an area in TD work that we need to encourage people to bring out more: tell us more *precisely* how your method works in the context you're doing it, because TD is so contextual.

I wondered if you have any comments that you might want to make about the relationships of TD knowledge in terms of their epistemology, ontology or metaphysics, or are those terms inappropriate to discussing TD knowledge?

I think those terms are very appropriate and, as I mentioned earlier, I come at TD work, the importance of TD work, from a perspective of wanting to try to solve things. And I know that there are many TD practitioners who are comfortable taking a problem and working with many disciplines and different methods and different frameworks, and focusing on solving problems. But sometimes I think there's not enough thinking about the theoretical underpinnings, the really metaphysical underpinnings of the work we're doing, and how that can scientifically justify trying to do something very complex like TD work. For example, I came up against this issue in trying to secure a grant from a foundation to do some complex work with patients who had Crohn's disease. This was to work on using artificial intelligence to create better mobile applications for these patients and for their physicians. I wanted to use a TD approach because many other things had not worked in the past, and because I knew that only TD approaches will work with complicated issues like the one that I wanted to address. However, the foundation pushed back; they said, The way it works with us is that you (the investigator) put into your grant application what the problem is—you define the problem, you define the solution and you predict the outcomes. And this is, of course, anathema to TD, in which you're supposed to work with all kinds of other people from different disciplines, stakeholders, including the end users to gradually define the problems together, the solutions together. Then, you're to test those over time and see which of the proposed solutions is going to work the best, and then come to a point where you have something that meets people's needs. All the relevant people are brought together in a TD process. But, this was exactly the *opposite* of the way most foundations and many governmental bodies that give out funding operate.

So, I had to make the case for why this (TD) was a better way to do things, because they were used to doing it the old way. What I did was make the case that the scientific foundation of TD is such that it *requires* using different methods, and that got me into issues of ontology—what reality is. On that point, I would subscribe to the ontological views similar to those of the physicist Basarab Nicolescu, who's done a lot of work in TD. He's built a lot of the scientific foundation that we use in TD. In his view, reality is not unidirectional or linear, but is best described as being made of multiple directions that are always changing in time and space. He likes to use the Internet as a good analogy because the Internet doesn't have a beginning or an end; it's constantly changing. For me, that's a good base for ontological thinking. And, if you subscribe to this perspective of how reality is, then this necessarily changes your thinking about epistemology or how you can understand reality, ways of knowing it. Again, the traditional view, the simpler linear view of ontology, fits better with traditional, natural science views of scientific enquiry, meaning that there are stable laws that cover reality and, once these laws are discovered through research, then you can pretty much generalise them to all contexts globally. As views of ontology began to change, as people began to think of it in a more complex, nonlinear way, then the ways of thinking about science or epistemology have become different, too. So, a lot of this happened during the scientific revolution of the last century, in which there was an understanding that, actually, reality being so complex, it's much more contextual, you can't just take a law and apply it everywhere in the world because things change, contexts are different. So, we had a lot of more epistemologies emerge during the last century, such as the human sciences, and that was an acknowledgment that, when humans are in the mix, it's very hard to predict what's happening, because humans are very contextual and changeable. So, human sciences includes the social sciences—those that really emerged strongly in last century—as a way to fill that gap.

The other thing that happened in the last century was that a big new branch of epistemology was developed called 'design sciences', and this is less well known to many of us who have traditional training in the sciences because we're very well trained in the natural sciences, chemistry, physics and that kind of thing, and also in human sciences: anthropology, sociology and other human sciences. But these don't really fill the whole gap because these sciences work mainly in either the present or the past, they are ways of studying what's happening in the present, or studying what happened in the past. But when we're trying to solve a complex problem, we're really trying to study the future. So, we're taking a problem that exists now, and we're trying to move forward into the future to try to address that. You can call TD work, then, 'future work'. That's really our big challenge. And the natural sciences and the human sciences, these first two epistemological branches—they don't really help us to do that well enough, so it's good that there's this third design science branch that emerged in the middle of the last century to help fill that gap.

What values do you consider appropriate to TD knowledge?

One value of this work is that stakeholder knowledge and knowledges of people from disciplines other than your own are equally valued. And, in many cases, they may be more valuable. I try to, in my work, put more value on what different stakeholders have to say and people from different disciplines have to say than on what I'm bringing in, because I know that's the place where I can personally really learn. And I try to foster the value of listening to others and having empathy with what they have to say, and trying to understand how that adds to knowledge of a problem and of a solution.

References

Fam, D., Neuhauser, L., & Gibbs, P. (2018). *Transdisciplinary theory, practice and education: The art of collaborative research and collective learning*. Cham: Springer.

Neuhauser, L. (2018). Practical and scientific foundations of transdisciplinary research and action. In D. Fam, L. Neuhauser, & P. Gibbs (Eds.), *Collaborative research and collective learning: Transdisciplinary research and practice*. Springer Press.

Neuhauser, L., & Pohl, C. (2014). Integrating transdisciplinary and translational concepts and methods into graduate education. In P. Gibbs (Ed.), *Transdisciplinary professional learning and practice*. New York: Springer.

Neuhauser, L., Richardson, D., Mackenzie, S., & Minkler, M. (2007). Advancing transdisciplinary and translational research practice: Issues and models of doctoral education in public health. *Journal of Research Practice, 3*(2), 19.

Neuhauser L., Wang, X., Hong, Y., Sun, X., Zong, Z., Shu, X., Mao, J., Lee E. W., & Aibe, S. (2018). Collaborative research and action: The China worker wellness project. In: D. Fam, L. Neuhauser, & P. Gibbs (Eds.), *Collaborative research and collective learning: Transdisciplinary research and practice*. Springer Press.

Chapter 9
Basarab Nicolescu

Basarab Nicolescu is an honorary theoretical physicist at the Centre National de la Recherche Scientifique (CNRS) in Paris. He is a Professor of the Babeş-Bolyai University in Romania and Extraordinary Professor of Stellenbosch University, South Africa. He is a member of the Romanian Academy and President and Founder of the International Center for Transdisciplinary Research and Studies (CIRET). He has lived in France since 1968.

His most influential books are: *Science, Meaning and Evolution—The Cosmology of Jacob Boehme* (1991); *Manifesto of Transdisciplinarity* (2002); *From Modernity to Cosmodernity: Science, culture, and spirituality* (2015); and *The Hidden Third* (2016).

We regard Basarab's position on transdisciplinarity to be captured in this short summary:

> The concept of levels of Reality, formulated in 1982, is the key concept of transdisciplinarity. The introduction of the levels of Reality induces a multidimensional and multi-referential structure of Reality, signifying the coexistence of complex plurality and open unity. Every level is characterised by its incompleteness; the laws governing this level are just a part of the totality of laws governing all levels. And even the totality of laws does not exhaust the entire Reality. We have also to consider the interaction between Subject and Object. The zone between two different levels and beyond all levels is one of non-resistance to our experiences, representations, descriptions, images and mathematical formulations. Knowledge is forever open.
>
> The unity of levels of Reality of the Object and its complementary zone of non-resistance defines the transdisciplinary Object. The unity of levels of Reality of the Subject and this complementary zone of non-resistance defines the transdisciplinary Subject. The zone of non-resistance plays the role of a third between the Subject and the Object, an interaction term that allows the unification of the transdisciplinary Subject and the transdisciplinary Object. This interaction term is called the Hidden Third. The ternary partition (Subject, Object and Hidden Third) is, of course, radically different from the binary partition (Subject vs. Object) of classical realism.

> According to Nicolescu, there are three axioms of the methodology of Transdisciplinarity:
>
> The ontological axiom: There are, in Nature and society and in our knowledge of Nature and society, different levels of Reality of the Object and, correspondingly, different levels of Reality of the Subject.
> The logical axiom: The passage from one level of Reality to another is ensured by the logic of the included middle.
> The epistemological axiom: The structure of the totality of levels of Reality or perception is a complex structure: every level is what it is because all the levels exist at the same time.

The following based upon an interview held with Basarab in June 2018, when he was in France.

My first question: Can you briefly describe your intellectual relationship to transdisciplinarity?

Well, I cannot answer to this question in a separate way, intellectually, from other aspects like spiritual and so on, but I will try. Okay, so intellectual: well, my starting point, because that was really the starting point from a long time, this means around the eighties, 1980, when I began to write about quantum physics, philosophical, a feature that struck me, struck me very much, is why there is such a huge separation between challenge in the visions of the world, like quantum vision and the reality of every day, mentality of the people. And that was the beginning of the whole story, so I was convinced more and more that this separation between the mentality of the people and what is restored in science, in culture, in everything is something which is in a basis of decline for civilisations…. Like a human being is the same from the time of all times, thousands and thousands and thousands years before Christ. Big civilisations, man was all the time the same. Revolution was external, social; and not internal. The human beings didn't face the challenge of the world, so that was my motivation for transdisciplinarity.

What do you take to be transdisciplinary practice?

Transdisciplinary practice for me has different stages. You know that I followed this international movement of transdisciplinarity essentially from 1985, when I wrote a book called *Us, the Particle of the World*, which is also about transdisciplinarity, so I began to correlate the methodology of transdisciplinarity. So the first stage of application of transdisciplinarity is to find new knowledge situated in the flux of information which is between disciplines. One thing; but there's a second level of practice and this is very useful, and that was applied from the beginning in transdisciplinarity.

Now, let me tell you without big vanity. When I was beginning to speak about transdisciplinarity, nobody heard me. I was alone, completely alone in France and outside France. It's true that my book had the prize of the French Academy, was recognised for quantum physics, was secular research—but the part with transdisciplinarity, very few people understood what I was talking about. So it was only in the nineties, essentially 1995, when we began to organise meetings and so on that the idea spread in the world. The first application was education; normal, because there you can apply this idea of a flux of information which is coming from different levels of reality and which integrates in the pupil, in the student, different complements, intellectual, instinctual and effective.

Now there is a second level of practice which is much more subtle, not very widespread, and I think is the challenge of the new stage of transdisciplinarity in the world. Now, to make this threshold, to pass this threshold, what is the question? More precisely, the challenge is to integrate first transdisciplinarity in yourself, in the transdisciplinary researcher. But practice, in order to involve the evolution of the human being, which I evoked in my first part of my intervention, what does that mean? Transdisciplinarity, of course it's not the spiritual way, transdisciplinarity is not the religious way, but it applies spiritual evolution, that's the part of transdisciplinarity. It's not religious, it's not a spiritual way but in practice, as we have to involve spiritual beings if we want transdisciplinarity to remain here at least for a few centuries; but the problem of vision remains. From where comes vision? From consultation of the interior world and exterior world. So I think this is now a second level of practice which is being carried out in a way in which the spiritual part of the researcher is involved and so the researcher becomes part of the knowledge.

There is a third part; there is three, now, in my system. There is a third level, which is very complicated to evoke without having the knowledge. It is about the Hidden Third. What I mean by the Hidden Third is this: the intermediate zone of knowledge between the subject and the object which allows the communication between the subject and the object. So it is a third part, independent from the subject and the object. I will say again, without any vanity, that's my main contribution to philosophy, the introduction of the Hidden Third. I didn't see it in other fields, just glimpses, Heidegger, other people, glimpses, but not really the role of the Hidden Third in knowledge. What means that? The Hidden Third is something which escapes by definition from analytical thinking. So, a classical man will say that's irrational. It's not probably irrational, because it's asked by reason; reason means proportion. The third part, the Hidden Third, is necessary in order to allow a bridge between two fundamental aspects of reality which are not recognised always.

Very few other than poets understand there is the unknown and the known. You see there is a dream, a fantasy, which motivated science and everything in the eighteenth, nineteenth, well twentieth century, which was that everything which is unknown will become known. What I developed in my theory, because this is a theory of transdisciplinarity, is the fact that there would be a part of reality which will remain unknown forever. What is that? Is it God? No, God is not in the framework of transdisciplinarity. What is that? It's something which is there in front of us and we have; and I think that was a big revelation in fact of the founders. Of the quantum mechanics, big thinkers like Heisenberg, what we do with unknown forever, is usually we reject it for we want to speak only about what is known. And I say, no. I always said no, but now I can formularise that. Now, we have to measure things with the unknown in order to bring the communication with what is known. In that kind we can have knowledge which is able to face the challenge of the twenty-first century. So, of three stages in practice, the Hidden Third is the more subtle thing because, for practising the Hidden Third, you have no tools for that except the extraordinary laboratory which is the interior being.

What is distinctive about the creation of transdisciplinary knowledge?

What is distinctive is first the acceptance of levels of reality in the subject and in the object. The usual disciplines and usual disciplinary thinking didn't accept that; they think that their discipline is the only thing which can present reality. The second point is to apply the unity of knowledge logic, which is not a classical logic, which is also distinctive. That's not easy, because people thought—and even today, let's be honest, between our colleagues and friends, even those who are involved in transdisciplinarity—sometimes they think there is a logic which is a data-alone logic, which is built in our brain. It's nonsense; we know that there are many logics and, by the beginning of the twentieth century, a lot of non-classical logics had already evolved. And that's natural, because in transdisciplinarity that's a distinctive feature, because you want to confront different aspects from different disciplines and they are necessarily contradictory. Being contradictory, you try to conciliate that. How you conciliate that? Applying the new logic; and I propose to use for transdisciplinarity a non-classical logic. When you put complexity together with levels of reality and which include the middle logic, there are many theories of complexity.

There are different understandings of complexity, but that the usual theories of complexity. Complexity acts in the same level of reality; it is horizontal. Where in transdisciplinarity there's a distinctive feature, complexity is acting vertically, is unifying different levels of reality. So complexity, as you know, doesn't mean complication, it means just internal penetration of different levels of knowledge. Interconnection. So these three things I said, levels of reality, including the middle logic and complexity, are the distinctive features of transdisciplinarity compared with everything we know today, and superimposed on all that is the thing on top which is giving a rational understanding—I underline—a rational understanding of what we are speaking about.

Do the notions of epistemology, ontology and metaphysics have any application to transdisciplinarity?

Well, not by themselves, of course, and I refuse the word metaphysics in transdisciplinarity. What I accept in transdisciplinarity is the dream which was always present for philosophers. What was the dream, if we try to simplify a little bit? For thousands and thousands and thousands of years, philosophy was to make a bridge between the beings, ontology, what is the being? With logics, how we apply theories and think and so on? And with epistemology, *works* with construction of systems of knowledge. And then, pretend—perhaps it's too much what I am saying but I have to say—it is the unifying ontology through levels of reality of object and subject with logics via non-classical logic and the use of complexity.

What kind of values do you associate with transdisciplinary knowing?

Yes, big question, and there were many debates in France's theory community when I said, in one of my papers, I think 10 years ago, there is no need, I said, no need for external values to be projected in process. And there was an explosion of papers because it was said, well, we need ethics, we need moral things. And I'm going, well, actually we need values. I said, we need not reintroduce values from external because values are generated in the dynamic way via the interplay of level sociality, logical think programming and complexity and the Hidden Third, which is the axis of all that. The Hidden Third is generating values, that's the key problem. Not by itself because, if the Hidden Third was alone, it is nothing. The Hidden Third needs reality, empirical reality. Reality is altering its law, by science, by thinking, by art, by dignity, by everything, means, and from this interaction is generating value. How is this possible? People have difficulty in understanding that. What I try to argue in all my work is that we are today confronted with a situation of knowledge in which there is no more fundamental basis for knowledge. Human beings, by fear, by despair, by I don't know what, have tried all ways to find a basis for knowledge, God was a basis. Dogmas were a basis. Physics was a basis. Based on my first experiences not as physicist but as a philosopher and trying to control to this many things I read, I studied. I arrived at the conclusion that the only reality is movement, everything is changed, the only basis of reality is movement. How can you can base on something which is all the time changing? You can, if they allow us to structure this 'movement', and these are the three aspects I spoke about. Level of sociality, included middle and complexity. So this means the human being is understanding this 'movement'.

The human being is not a separated, like Einstein thought, from reality. The human being is not a kind of god who looks at reality and decides everything about reality which is external. It's a difficult concept, I must say, because of many hidden ideological, religious, philosophical assumptions. When people react about values, they bring a lot of prejudices with them and they don't know that. The first thing, first step, when we speak about transdisciplinarity practice is to discover what are the hidden prejudices when we assert something. Only then we can begin to value.

What do You consider to be the conditions and barriers for the development of transdisciplinarity?

Yeah, barriers are everywhere. Barriers are institutional because institutions are based on a system of education and research which is modelled on the nineteenth century, even now twentieth century, in most of the countries—there are exceptions, of course. They have right results in specialisation but they give no place for transdisciplinarity, because they say it's not efficient. Efficient for what? For speciality research, which is honest, yes. Speciality research is one thing, very useful but it's not sufficient. Transdisciplinary research is very useful but it's not sufficient by itself; we have to combine disciplines and the transdisciplinary approach. And I will say: if institutions do not see that, they will not survive. Present universities, I predict, perhaps I will no longer be alive when this will happen, but it will happen, universities will disappear one after the other because they will be replaced by technological institutions. Engineers will be everywhere. So, I'm not joking. But in many cases, it's a condition for survival. Transdisciplinarity is not a luxury, it's not just intellectual play, and it is a necessity if we want to face the complexity of our world. Our world is so complex that it cannot be reduced to an all-disciplinary fragmented framework.

Now: another barrier which is much more subtle and much more dangerous, which is inside, inside us. We are constituted by many things but, in our thinking, we have conscious thoughts and we have unconscious thoughts, subconscious thoughts. And we don't know, in fact even big thinkers and big researchers, that we are manipulated by our unconscious representations: it's a big [issue] for me and I have verified this myself, which is the easiest way to verify. So that's a huge barrier. When I... I'm not saying that I'm a free man but, for me, freedom is addressing these internal barriers, so how this can be done?

The classical way is to engage in a religious movement, in a spiritual movement and so on. I would say you have another way which is adopted through the twenty-first century, which is a spirituality without dogmas. This means a new kind of spirituality, open spirituality, open to all religions, all spiritualities, all cultural movements, open, and which allows us to become conscious about our internal limitation. Psychoanalysis is also very good for that, and I was amazed to discover in the work of Heisenberg how much he helped to shape psychoanalysis at this time. Heisenberg said that there's a science of spirit. It's incredible, and it's very nice because he felt that we have to clarify first the internal thing, inside us, before accepting something about reality, externally. Pauli was a bright man in the same direction, of course he was under the influence of Jung but, in any case, he had resolved thinking of this way and the unconscious part of thinking was basic for Pauli to understand what I am speaking about; we physicians, for example, when we speak about physical laws. So, I think the internal values are inside and for that I think that one of the hugest challenge for the future, in the transdisciplinarity movement, again what I'm saying, now, is not a question of 1 year, 2 years, it can be ten, can be twenty, is the correlation of a new study, new transdisciplinary theory of consciousness. For me it is the crucial, one of the crucial aspects. I became involved in the research of some theories after staying at Michigan University and we produced a paper, in collaboration with Arthur Versluis, in which we gain some glimpses about what we think about this new transdisciplinary theory of consciousness.

What present theories of consciousness are saying is that there are small things inside the brain, quantum kinds of things, which are giving the basis of thought. I think it's a wrong direction. It's the wrong direction because, again from the transdisciplinary point of view, you have to demonstrate in that new theory of consciousness, what is unknown against what is known. And this is possible only if you introduce the methodology of transdisciplinarity in a theory of consciousness. I think it's a big challenge.

References

Nicolescu, B. (1991). *Science, meaning and evolution—The cosmology of Jacob Boehme* (R. Baker, Trans.). New York: Parabola Books.
Nicolescu, B. (2002). *Manifesto of transdisciplinarity* (K.-C. Voss, Trans.). New York: SUNY.
Nicolescu, B. (2015). *From modernity to cosmodernity: Science, culture, and spirituality*. Albany: SUNY.
Nicolescu, B. (2016). *The hidden third* (W. Garvin, Trans.). New York: Quantum Prose.

Chapter 10
Christian Pohl

Christian Pohl, with a PhD in environmental sciences and a habilitation degree from the University of Bern, is Co-Director of the Transdisciplinarity Lab (TdLab) of the Department of Environmental Systems Science at ETH Zurich (www.tdlab.usys. ethz.ch). TdLab is in charge of the department's transdisciplinary case-study teaching, runs transdisciplinary projects and develops theories and methods of transdisciplinary research. Christian Pohl studied environmental science, followed by a doctoral thesis on uncertainty in environmental assessments. As a postdoc, he moved to the field of science studies and analysed interdisciplinary and transdisciplinary research. Over the past decade he has contributed to the development of the theory and practice of transdisciplinary research, specifically in the field of sustainable development. He has written extensively on transdisciplinarity and, of his works, those which we consider his most influential are: *Principles for Designing Transdisciplinary Research* (2007); *Handbook of Transdisciplinary Research* (2008) and *What is Progress in Transdisciplinary Research?* (2011).[1]

We regard Christian's position on transdisciplinarity to be captured in this short summary:

> Pohl has located his understanding of transdisciplinarity within, broadly, three Concepts:
>
> Concept A, transdisciplinarity is research that transcends and integrates disciplinary paradigms in order to address socially (as opposed to academically) relevant issues. The rationale for transcending and integrating disciplinary paradigms is that academic knowledge, organised from a disciplinary perspective, has to be reorganised and re-assessed in order to be relevant for addressing socially relevant issues.
>
> Concept B of transdisciplinarity starts from Concept A and adds the inclusion of non-academic actors (i.e. doing participatory research) as a feature. The inclusion of

---

[1] See https://scholar.google.ch/citations?user=E1_0iCoAAAAJ&hl=de for a list of Pohl's publications.

> the non-academic actors takes up the discussion on Mode 2 knowledge production that was influential in Europe over the past decade. Mode 2 knowledge production takes place in the context of application and includes knowledge and stakeholders from science, civil society and the private and the public sectors.
>
> Concept C of transdisciplinarity adds the search for a unity of knowledge to Concept A. The overall aim is—as with Concept A—to reorganise academic knowledge in order to make it useful for addressing socially relevant issues. Knowledge is reorganised by developing the basis for a general viewpoint or perspective, beyond all disciplines. Once such a fundamental structure of knowledge beyond all disciplines is revealed, the socially relevant issues can be structured, analysed and processed from that viewpoint (2011: 619–620).

The following based upon an interview held with Christian in June 2018, when he was in Scotland.

Could You explore what interested you in transdisciplinarity?

When I studied environmental sciences, I had the impression that we students were expected to use knowledge of different disciplines and to collaborate with actors of different sectors of society to solve real problems, but nobody told us how to do this. Towards the end of my PhD I was fellow at the Collegium Helveticum, at that time directed by the science studies scholars Helga Nowotny and Yehuda Elkana. Helga Nowotny invited me to join a research project on socially robust knowledge. I thought, okay, now I should research what really bothers me: transdisciplinarity. The first intellectual aim—as a Postdoc—was to understand transdisciplinarity by analysing TD projects in the field of sustainable development. Four years later, I had the chance to become founding Co-Director of the transdisciplinarity net of the Swiss Academies of Arts and Sciences. This was a double shift, from a research institution to one that supports community building; from understanding TD research to supporting people in doing it. In the transdisciplinarity net, and together with Gertrude Hirsch Hadorn and others we develop handbooks, organised conferences and, later, also collected methods to support co-production of knowledge. And now, I am back where I studied and teach students in how to run a TD project.

I think that's the intellectual relationship. I got interested because I was expected to do transdisciplinary projects, but nobody told me how to do so. I thought, okay, I should try to build theories and find case studies and methods that support people in doing transdisciplinary research.

What is the difference between transdisciplinary practice and disciplinary practice?

Let me answer the question by how we teach transdisciplinary practice in one of our courses, a year-long Bachelor course with 140–150 students in the curriculum of programme of environmental sciences. These are BSc students in their first year who don't have the kind of disciplinary expertise usually said to be one pillar of transdisciplinary research, meaning they have to become 'novice experts', to be ready for transdisciplinary exchange. The students become 'novice experts' in the first semester by analysing one of the six aspects of the overall topic. For instance, this year's topic was building houses from houses and the recycling of concrete. Some of the students would go into the topic's legal aspects, some into the technologies, others in the material aspects of concrete, others in the costs and benefits. I think that's a first element of TD practice. TD practice means addressing an issue from different perspectives in order to grasp its complexity.

A second element is integration, bringing the different perspectives together, not necessarily in a huge synthesis or consensus, but by connecting them. For that, we mix the students who studied one of six aspects in the first semester in new groups of six for the second semester, one student from each aspect. As a first exercise they have to draw a rich picture—that's soft systems methodology—to develop a first overall impression of the topic. So, different perspectives are important for TD practice, but also to connect them to an overall picture.

A third element of TD practice is going beyond the overall analysis and trying to focus on manageable problems. We do that by asking students to identify and specify 'small problems' within the overall picture. Problems, issues, challenges, situations whatever the terminology is you like. Taken from the viewpoint of sustainable development could be improved. Our environmental science students are usually strong in analysis. They want to get the whole picture, and also to keep it. For some of them it is a challenge to focus on one specific 'small problem', but if you want to get practical, you have to leave the whole picture perspective and select particular parts of it to be changed, such as the laws, the prices, the technologies, the perceptions of architects or house builders.

A fourth element is to come up with solutions that are at the same time feasible and have the indented effect in the overall system. For the feasibility part we use design thinking: Students brainstorm ideas, develop prototypes and test them with stakeholders. To keep the balance between the whole picture and the 'small' solution or problem, students have to display the overall picture in a simple qualitative system model. They connect their solution back to the overall picture by modelling what effects it will have in the overall system. This is to make students aware that interventions in systems might not work as planned and might have unintended consequences. That's part of TD practice, too, some things don't behave as you thought they would.

A fifth element of TD practice, at least in the European sustainability related concept of transdisciplinarity, is stakeholder involvement To my perception this element came up in the nineteen-nineties, and gained traction with the book of Gibbons, Nowotny and colleagues, *The New Production of Knowledge.* Mode 2 knowledge production in the context of application and socially robust knowledge meets TD research, which at that time in Switzerland was mainly conceptualised as different disciplines collaborating to solve sustainability problems. In the Europe sustainability related TD concept, stakeholder involvement (the idea that to have impact in society, those concerned have to be included in the transdisciplinary research process) has become a key characteristic of transdisciplinarity, up to the point where some see it as the one element that differentiates interdisciplinarity from transdisciplinarity. In my view that's a reductionist understanding of transdisciplinarity. However, in our course we ask students to identify the stakeholder groups that would be affected by the solutions they propose. Later in the course students have to present and discuss the prototypes of their solution with representatives of these stakeholder groups. Some stakeholders might find the solution unnecessary, others might want to implement it right away. So, students have to deal with the different stakeholder groups and their interests.

Coming back to your question and taking our course as example, I see at least five elements that distinguish TD from disciplinary practice: Analysing an issue from plural perspectives, relating the perspectives to develop an overall picture, framing manageable 'small' problems in the overall picture, developing feasible solutions while keeping an eye on unintended side effects and involving stakeholders in the process of knowledge production.

How do you help the students to develop a means of resolving different stakeholder views on their solution?

We mainly use methods of design thinking for that purpose. An important step in design thinking is formulating a problem statement, in which you describe the problem from the perspective of the stakeholder. You try to reframe it from the viewpoint of his or her needs. After identifying relevant stakeholders by a stakeholder analysis, students have to develop problem statements for the 3–4 most important stakeholders. Formulating problem statements means to dig deep into the respective interests and perspectives. Only after that students will brainstorm possible solutions. I guess our assumption is, if you first dig deep into the stakeholders' diverse interest and framings, and only then brainstorm solutions, the diverse interest will affect what you brainstorm.

Later in the process the students present the prototyped solutions to the stakeholders and ask for feedback. We make students aware that this is at the same time a test of the problem statement they formulated, and that the problem statement might require adaptations depending on the stakeholder's reaction to the prototype. So, we try to support students to deal with the diverse interests by asking them to dig deep into the stakeholders' viewpoints and by asking them to test their concepts of stakeholders in face-to-face exchanges.

Is there such a thing as TD Knowledge, transdisciplinary knowledge, as distinct from knowledge per se? Is transdisciplinarity in the knowledge or is in the process of generating knowledge?

I think what is very specific for TD knowledge compared to disciplinary knowledge— and know I refer to Ludwig Fleck's theory of thought styles and thought collectives— is that usually, if you're in a discipline, you belong to a particular thought collective and thought style. The topics you study, the research you do, the expression you use, the questions you consider relevant, the methods you apply, they are all accepted in and will be approved by your thought style.[2] As they are the usual way of doing

---

[2] See *What is Progress in Transdisciplinary Research* (2011), where Pohl discusses how collaboration and integration in transdisciplinary research can be understood through thought styles.

research in your discipline, you will not realise that they're full of assumptions and value judgements, e.g. about what acceptable evidence is or what legitimate sources of insights are. As soon as you move into a TD context all this given conditions collapse. Not the conditions per so, but the collective acceptance of them. That is, in a TD context you have several thought styles based on different ideas about, for instance, what a fact is or when something is proven enough to be trusted. So, the process of exchange gains in importance, because in a TD context you have to explain and justify everything that you don't have to explain and justify in your home discipline because it's standard. Tons of standards, some of which you don't consider being a standard of your discipline alone, but of science in general. I think that's a huge difference between a disciplinary exchange and a TD exchange. So, I don't think there is TD knowledge as separate from disciplinary knowledge. But in a TD context the different knowledges come without the supporting 'corset' of disciplinary assumptions and therefore need a lot of further explanations in order to be adequately included in knowledge co-production process.

What, then, makes things true?

I guess the consequences are that in a TD context there are different truths. If there are different thought styles, then there are different concepts of truth. For some thought collectives it might be a question of logical conclusions, for others of double-blind test, a model able to reproduce historical data or a set of interviews reaching saturation. What makes all of this true? I don't think that there is, or that there should be, a consensus about the criteria for truth within transdisciplinary projects. I think there should be a plurality of viewpoints and a plurality of truth criteria. They should coexist during the TD process. As soon as you want to publish insights gained in this process in your disciplinary thought collective, then you have probably to relate to the respective criteria again.

If I look at the practice side of a TD process—the students who present their solutions to stakeholders—then I think the burning question is not 'Is it true?', but rather 'Does it work?' I'm not sure what kind of truth criteria that is. But for me, always if a stakeholder from practice says 'That's a great idea, I buy it' and some of them bought ideas, literally, from our students, then I have to say: 'That's just great, I don't know if it is true, but it seems to work for practice'.

Do the notions of epistemology, ontology and metaphysics have any different interpretation within the *Rubric* of transdisciplinarity or not? Are those tools as useful?

You know, I'm a constructivist and my knowledge about ontology is shallow. What I consider relevant is epistemology. For me that's the way of how people perceive things. And the thought-styles and thought-collective approach is one way to explain why different disciplines and different stakeholders perceive things differently, they have different epistemologies. I'm personally not convinced we should establish a shared epistemology in a TD process. I think we should keep the plurality of epistemologies as long as the TD project takes. I think that's the role of epistemology in transdisciplinarity. You have to become aware that they're different epistemologies; you don't have to become aware of that fact in a disciplinary project.

What are the conditions, environments that are needed for TD activities to thrive and what is the inverse? What are the barriers?

Referring back to my Swiss context, I think universities that are less organised in disciplines, both in research and in education, provide more opportunities for TD activities. I am based in an engineering school. As far as I understand that's different from a large comprehensive university that are rather organised in traditional disciplines. My school is fast in creating new departments and closing down older ones. The 'newer' departments are organised around thematic fields rather than disciplines. Examples are 'environmental systems science' or 'health science and technology'. This is in principle a good environment for transdisciplinary research. I'm less sure about the tenure track career system. There, the h-index, and the question in what journals you publish matters. Then, all of a sudden, it matters to what disciplinary thought collective you belong and how often your publications are quoted by this collective. Then you are somehow back in a discipline.

In Switzerland, I think the funding opportunities support TD projects. The Swiss National Science Foundation provides policy-driven funding schemes that even ask for TD research. And there is a thematically open funding scheme for ID or TD projects. Also, some of the private foundations are very open to TD projects because their purpose is to tackle specific societal problems.

Are they interested in transdisciplinarity or are they interested in a solution? or to accommodate transdisciplinarity, especially if it gets a solution?

I think you're right, they're interested in the solution. However, over the last years transdisciplinarity has made its way on their radar and they see, oh, that's the kind of research we should done. At least some of them.

Another barrier could be publishing. Twenty years ago I would have said places to publish TD project results are rare. I don't think that's true any longer. The number of publications on transdisciplinary projects is growing, there are journals, rather good journals, where you can publish the results of transdisciplinary research; and there are journals that publish about transdisciplinarity as a method or approach.

A main barrier for transdisciplinary projects are people who are 'orthodox', who believe that their discipline or expertise is the only right one. I think you can't work with them in transdisciplinary projects. People have to be open-minded, interested in exchange with other disciplines or experts of other societal sectors; they have to be interested in spending time with others. I think the open-mindedness is crucial. Which is funny, because the different schools of TD are not as open to each other, as they should.

How do you develop transdisciplinary solutions without creating another hierarchy of knowledge and power?

Do we create new hierarchies? I guess we are a bit naïve in that respect, because what we want to create is a group collaboration inside of the hierarchies of disciplines and the hierarchies between science and other sectors of society. However, we also see, how to say, hierarchies as a tool that can be useful. Sometimes people think, for instance, that integration means all people sitting around the table and integrating all the time. I think that we are, in our approach, more pragmatic. We say, okay, that's one option of how to strive for integration. And if you have good reasons why this is the adequate approach for integration then go for it. Another way is to put everything into a model and the model integrates. The model has a specific language, and will exclude and include things, and in that way has the power to filter information. But perhaps for what is at stake, this it's the right approach. In another case, it might make sense to delegate the task of integration to a specific subgroup or to one person.

I think we try to be pragmatic and also not to be afraid of hierarchies. Rather we aim at making hierarchies explicit. Once they are 'on the table' a TD group can decide whether this is the way to go for the next days or weeks and, if necessary, to adapt it. It's about being flexible, pragmatic, to try out things and, if they don't work, go back. I think that's also how we try to deal with hierarchies.

References

Hadorn, G. H., Hoffman-Riem, H., Biber-Klemm, S., Grossenbacher-Mansuy, W., Joye, D., Pohl, C., et al. (Eds.). (2008). *Handbook of transdisciplinary research*. Cham: Springer.

Pohl, C. (2011). What is progress in transdisciplinary research? *Futures, 37*(10), 1159–1178.

Pohl, C., & Hirsch Hadorn, G. (2007). *Principles for designing transdisciplinary research*. Munich: Swiss Academies of Arts and Sciences.

Part III
Reflections and Case Study Appendix

Chapter 11
Thematics Reflections

The objective of this book is not to identify a universal theme that runs through the works of all the educational thinkers and practitioners featured in its chapters. Having read their views, it is obvious that transdisciplinarity is far too rich in realities for that to be worthwhile. What this short summary attempts is to cast a light on some of the key similarities in the themes that our thinkers have shown us and to share them with readers. We do not do this in a mechanical way, by tabulating responses against common headings used, but by taking a high-level discursive view of the conceptualisation of transdisciplinary knowledge that we have been offered. Diversity is to be wondered at, and enhances our thinking. This embraces the diversity, not the acculturalisation of that diversity into a single, colonising treatise. The thinkers whom we have heard from in this book offer such insights. The themes developed have a patterning—a relational embodiment—and are clearly not extensive. They are what we, as editors, take from the text, and we hope that readers are able to see these as indicative only.

Complexity

The interwoven nature of complexity is manifest in the messy; or, as Brown would have it, 'wicked' problems which are clearly evident in the knowledge that emerges from engagement with such problems. We go further and argue that complexity is used to understand and engage with these problems. Transdisciplinarity emerges from what Kate calls 'complexity and interconnectedness'. Concerns for a unity of knowledge, bounded by a reality of consistency, and is necessarily dissipated into a relational multi-reality world of complex, dynamic, open systems where truth, trust and knowledge mingle with hope, compassion and dignity. This combination reaches out to the real world and rhizomatically results in an understanding that differs in form and structure from those available through disciplinary reason, encumbered by the hegemonies that support the power enshrined in the epistemological principles that give authority and exclusivity to a form of knowledge as truth. Such engagements, by their very nature, are interactions among multiple actors, giving rise to value conflicts and contradictions. These conflicts can result in power struggles, not emergent knowledge. However, as Sue offers us, by its very nature transdisciplinarity gives rise to value conflicts and contradictions. These conflicts can result in power struggles but, if confronted and managed, power can be turned into positive energy collectives. Indeed, Basarab places complexity within his three axioms, arguing that transdisciplinarity is a necessity if we want to face up to the complexity of our world.

Plurality

Plurality has been seen to be a feature of much of what is proposed in the views captured in this book. Truth is relative to the context to which it contributes. It is neither constant nor absolute. Christian maintains that there should be a consensus about the criteria for truth within transdisciplinary projects. He argues for a plurality of viewpoints, a plurality apparently connected to the viewpoints, and a plurality of truth criteria. These will exist, or coexist, during this process.

Temporal fluidity

Fluidity of time refers to certainty in the known past, the knowable present and the imagined future. Gray talks of motion, Kate of flux and Linda of ontological change. The very notion of our world, seen through the lens of transdisciplinarity, can be both in and as change. Our knowledge frameworks are losing their power in our more complex and changing circumstances. This requires a new way of striving to be, to seek a flexible self and shorter fixes; not the mythical change that brought us to stasis but change that, itself, is changing. This needs less archaeology of knowledge and more a disaggregated way that involves people in finding solutions. It means us forgoing the certainty of the knowledge hegemony of the Western Enlightenment, instead questioning it, paying more attention to the real and deep knowledge of those affected by both the immediacy of problems and, more importantly, the sustained change that these solutions provide. In this, temporality is considered as an extended present where linear, emotional, rational and social time all merge, such temporal space and the realities that it contains is the context when we speak of transdisciplinarity. It is where the presence of agency is woven with expectations for the future, built on a genuine engagement with the past, and not solely by investigators but by those affected. This will evolve into a form of dignity that ought to be at the core of transdisciplinary action.

Normative changes

Scientific knowledge and technical expertise continue to emerge from disciplines and see problems outside the complexity of their realities. The reality of our current anthroposphere needs to be supported, reviewed and integrated. The bio-complexity of our long-term well-being; our social systems that have assuaged the spirituality that underpins our ontological stance and our morality, which offers us a reason to become, have all become corrupted under the powerful discourses of hate, envy and greed, breeding unfettered on narratives of self-interest and selfishness. Both Basarab and Christian ask you to reflect to understand our own prejudice and values which determine our thought styles and thus the way in which we might inauthentically see the world and how through transdisciplinarity practice we might see it different through the light of authenticity.

Educative change

Val's quote about her actions 'tearing the university down, brick by brick' has a negative connotation yet what is clear in her abductive agency, and that of others, is not destruction but the renewal through a synthesis of what was the cultural norm with the innovative patterning, discovery and positivity that have taken transdisciplinarity from the peripheral to the central comprising curriculum development, research skill and practical impact. The issues of educative and collaborative learning from all parties within the problem are evident in what we have read by our thinkers. As Kate discusses, it involves recognising our disciplinary roots and then going into the background of that disciplinary training and our assumptions, not forgoing them but trying to look afresh. Gray offers a form of curriculum guidance for those seeking the development of transdisciplinary knowledge which includes the nurturing of the disposition of curiosity, risk-taking, ambiguity and precision, combined with expansiveness. For Basarab the challenge in transdisciplinarity education is a new transdisciplinary theory of consciousness.

Transdisciplinary being

Becoming, then, is creating practical knowledge that is testable in the world of practice; it is the fusion of passive and active causal powers in the transdisciplinary nexus of the Hidden Third. It creates an understanding of how the potentiality of being can be made manifest as poetic performance in the arena of emergent realities. Freedom resides in our choice to act on our potential, and potentialities are aligned with the properties of the thing that determines its powers to act. Thus, not all the properties of a thing are equally important.

The exploration of our being provides the potential for us to understand our life project and to seek it. It is not deterministic, and neither is it unencumbered; it requires a blend of knowledges and realities so we might have the power to reflect and deliberate on the impact to be achieved by our actions. Most importantly, this time-space manifold is not static but in constant motion; a flow, with complexity and causation. In it, any replication of empirical, closed-system analysis occurs only in abstraction, for this flow of realities is conceived as an open system in which possible worlds emerge and realities are perceived and lost in time and space, dependent on the location of the becoming being. It is in this primary sense of becoming as potentiality, as energy, that there is capacity to bring about change in another thing or in itself. Linda talks of transformative change in the process of transdisciplinary projects. This links to the theme of educative progress.

Appendix
Louise McWhinnie—My UTS Experience

The final chapter is an interview with the founding Dean of the Faculty of Transdisciplinary Innovation at University of Technology Sydney (UTS), Professor Louise McWhinnie. We include this to illustrate the feasibility of successfully building, integrating and nurturing transdisciplinarity at the core of an institution's mission. It is an example of how an idea that is innovative, creative and practical can achieve the goals of students, academic and society in the complex world within which higher education must function. Louise's account of how this was achieved in UTS is an illuminating and fitting close to the argument in this book. The interview took place in March 2019 in Sydney.

Context

I am the inaugural Dean of the Faculty of Transdisciplinary Innovation at UTS. Six years ago, and prior to the establishment of the faculty, UTS set out to understand not only the technological revolution but what it recognised was an ideas revolution, and the first transdisciplinary course was designed. It formed the basis of what, 3 years later, would become the first new faculty at UTS in over 20 years, and the only transdisciplinary faculty of its kind in Australia.

The course that launched this was called the Bachelor of Creative Intelligence and Innovation (BCII) and was conceived as a point of academic differentiation and distinction for the University and its students. It was at this time that, as a university of technology, UTS was also articulating that reputational growth must result from leadership in innovation through academic ownership of a clear link between creativity and technology, at a time in which the future of work was rapidly changing. Such a link stemmed from the University's close affiliation with industry and its perceived need for different types of graduates: ones who could transcend traditional disciplinary borders. What these graduates were to be, and how they should be educationally prepared, could not, however, be articulated by industry—they simply identified the necessity for different forms of graduates for a fast and vastly changing world.

A number of other universities were already exploring the potential of design thinking, but our approach was driven instead by the belief that we needed to develop a more far-sighted vision for an academic and educational revolution. The result was the intertwining of two degrees, one disciplinary and one transdisciplinary, so both components immediately informed the other without altering the core degree structure but with an educational model that remained industry informed. The BCII was designed to immerse students in a wide range of diverse disciplinary practices so that they both experienced and observed them in action, implementing (and interpreting) these practices within the context of assessable challenges.

From first degree to faculty

Its conception as a combined degree was always core to the BCII's potential success, and it launched in combination with 18 different degrees, a number that has now grown to 24. Clear also was the recognition that innovation occurred within, but also across, between and beyond singular disciplines, and that creativity could grow from a base of disciplinary knowledge yet it never existed in isolation simply for its own sake. The creation of a graduate with disciplinary depth, but also creative and technological breadth, was vital in this.

The faculty now has 10 programmes spanning innovation, creative intelligence, emergent technology, data science and new forms of visualisation and animation, from diploma to degree, and from masters to PhD. These programmes and our way of working forefront critical and creative thinking, problem posing and solving, innovation and invention, complexity and entrepreneurship, and all engage students in not only future-focused learning but building in them flexibility and capabilities to be able to adapt to, frame and lead future change. The faculty is one of eight across the University, and the only one formed beyond the model of singular or conjoined disciplines that exists within most other universities. We might be one faculty, but our role is to work across, between and beyond the silos of single disciplines.

The first course that was formed (the BCII), and would later create a basis for the faculty, was created at the intersection of industry desiring more from universities, but also, it appears, a particular group in a new generation of students who were seeking more from their university experience. With the first degree launched at speed and with limited marketing, it received approximately 1500 applications in that first year. That, of course, has since been eclipsed for, within 3 years, the BCII became the second most applied-for undergraduate degree at the University with, as a mark of popularity, some of the highest entry scores it was possible for students to achieve.

Build it right, and they will come?

Having immersed ourselves in a very fast and deep transdisciplinary dive in the conceiving of and design of the BCII course in 2013, we took it to market with the feeling that this was the course its authors all 'wished we had studied'. It immediately attracted students that didn't want to confine their curiosity to a single professional path at the age of 18. That wasn't a lack of decisiveness on their part, it was genuine curiosity and desire for a different type of education. Students were clearly indicating that they were seeking breadth from their learning experience, in addition to the depth of a single discipline. They were curious and, in many ways, we tapped into these genuinely curious students who wanted more than just a university education, instead seeking a different university 'experience' that would also provide differentiation in a competitive but disciplinary often-generic graduate world. I genuinely believe that at the point of time at which we attracted our first cohort of students, we did so not on our ability to demonstrate the conceptual quality of the course (with no precedent in the Australian higher education sector and an inability to name the jobs that they would graduate to), but by offering an alternative university learning experience model for those students who knew what they didn't want but didn't know what they wanted. Now, of course, recruiting students is different in that we have a demonstrated concept with proof of outcomes (successful graduates).

On reflection, I think that the reason why the academic staff have such a particular affection for the students of that first-ever BCII cohort is because we found very bright and curious students, with high ATARs, who were willing not only to be risk-takers in their choice of study but also in their intelligence and belief in their abilities. They were also willing to take the risk of a 'deep dive' journey into a new conceptual space with academic staff who were also in a state of exploration. On reflection, what was also vital to the BCII's immediate success was that the transdisciplinary degree was a double degree, enabling students to take a risk on such a course of study with the safety net of their usual core degree.

Taking this metaphor a little further, I have also wondered if the perception of a safety net made the students more willing to be trapeze artists in their BCII education by embracing the risk of mistake and failure in their exploration; alternatively, whether it became a trampoline, offering students the potential to springboard from the BCII into new and expanded contexts within their core disciplines. On reflection, however, this raises the question of if, in launching the first degree, we created a desire in prospective students for a new type of education or whether the response was a result of us delivering what they had always been seeking but didn't know existed.

Transdisciplinarity: An irony-free zone

The irony of within 3 years of the creation of the first programme being formed as a 'faculty', when our remit was to challenge and transcend disciplinary boundaries and faculty silos, was not lost on me. Being formed as the first new university faculty in over two decades sent a very clear statement from the vice-chancellor across both the institution and the sector. In our first 3 years we were safely housed in a disciplinary faculty prior to being formed as a stand-alone faculty. In most universities, we would all too often have been established simply as a department or centre, which in essence would define it as not being at the centre for the university but, instead, an outlier, an experiment. It was that visible university commitment that was pivotal: enabling transdisciplinary studies to be represented at the top table for all of the important conversations and on an equal footing with existing faculties. In this decision, the UTS chancellery provided transdisciplinarity with a recognition that it could have taken years to otherwise earn.

I also attribute the faculty's formation to its presence at a particular moment in time; a time in which UTS, as a young university, was finding its feet and establishing its confidence, recognising its strengths as well as its abilities and, importantly, its right to be different. With that bravado, as a young (non-sandstone or redbrick) university, it was a perfect combination of institutional vision and commitment combined with agility.

Moving beyond the university

Ninety-five per cent of the subjects we deliver across all of our programmes are formed around industry partnerships and their challenges, with over 600 highly engaged and active industry partnerships supporting and engaging with subjects and activities. Attracting such active and vital partners and managing and maintaining these partnerships has been highly rewarding and core to the educational experience for staff and students. To secure this number and quality of partners has been the result of their attraction to the quality of the management of their partnership, as well as the level of engagement and new forms of thinking that they can access, which prove to be both refreshing and of significant value to them.

Watching students move beyond the traditions and structures of their own disciplinary space is exciting to witness, as is the creation of outcomes that singular disciplines could not achieve. What has become clear is that for a significant number of students the BCII, rather than being secondary, has become the primary degree in their double degree combination. Transdisciplinarity, and how that structures their ability to deal with complexity, structures their ability to think in new ways and builds new capabilities, and has become the determinant in their future pathways.

I am now in the exciting position to be able to witness how a transdisciplinary undergraduate (and now postgraduate) educational experience translates in new ways into an applied world beyond the theoretical dreams we had for a new form of student learning. With our first student cohort completing their university study in 2017, their transition to employment, and the employers' transition to the graduates, is proving fascinating. For transdisciplinary graduates, group work is obviously their primary means of working, not the by-product it can all too often be in their core degree learning. Students understand how to work between, across and beyond disciplinary approaches and knowledge, and how to probe complexity rather than address complicated or complex challenges. They understand failure and how to pivot, and can see and place their core discipline and its knowledge within a broader context. They also, very importantly, understand how they socialise their own discipline, and so how others socialise theirs.

Looking back over 6 years (Hurdles: Vaulting, Clearing, Tripping and Running Around Them)

I would love to say that I knew that this would all become what it has, but that would be a retrospective writing of history that I cannot claim. Designing courses and learning experiences without historical or disciplinary precedent has been challenging and rewarding. However, from the start, there was a sense with the University that this was something different, and it wasn't just for difference's sake. It was a genuine journey into what education could become, even at undergraduate level, in a space of exploration and uncertainty.

Don't for a moment assume that this journey has been smooth, or that establishing the first transdisciplinary programme with multiple cross-university degrees, establishing new programmes or a transdisciplinary faculty has been or is easy. There are many challenges, and an entire book could be written on institutional and sector-wide implementation and measurement hurdles that need to be jumped, or at times swerved around. I sometimes think of these six transdisciplinary years of my 26 years working in higher education as being full of glorious moments, and yet also resembling a marathon, run at speed with trip hazards.

We are now both now a faculty and at times an anti-faculty—expected to take risks, but at times judged through education and research against measures used for traditional, often more risk-averse, disciplinary measures of success. This is both a genuine joy and also at times a frustration, but a challenge that I was always aware would exist. Having been an associate dean in one of the University's disciplinary faculties for a number of years, I was fully conversant with the people, politics and systems that would have to be negotiated, persuaded and occasionally manipulated. Still in an initial development phase, possibly maybe still able to be termed a start-up, certainly a work in progress, the faculty is established but still has a long way to go. In this marathon run at speed, it is probably only now, in writing this that I can reflect upon what, with hindsight, I would wish to have known 6 years ago.

I would probably immediately tell myself to **locate the right staff**, and warn myself that many people express their desire to move into the transdisciplinary space. Take the time to talk to them, listen carefully and ensure that they wish to move *into* transdisciplinary education and research, and not instead jump *out of* their present teaching and research environment. Locating **the right course directors** has also been vital, with individuals with the ability to internally and externally articulate course and faculty vision as well as the significant social and industry shifts that make transdisciplinarity such a vital component within a future-focused space. Articulation and persuasion, particularly to initial sceptics, is fundamental in entry into a transdisciplinary space, with the expectation that it will engage broadly, unlike more traditional and established disciplines.

In establishing the first course (BCII), we identified and engaged with a small number of very particular **academic staff from across disciplines and all of the institutional faculties**. Their knowledge and thoughtfulness at an early stage were vital to the conceptualisation of courses, allowing what was created to go far beyond what would otherwise have been achieved. Such engagement resulted in input into the early stage of educational development by highly regarded cross-university staff who, in turn, also became ambassadors and champions back into their own faculties. An unexpected but gratifying bonus was that this engagement resulted in a significant number of these champions also engaging in the delivery of the first-ever subject. That, in itself, exposed such staff to new ways of thinking and new educational models of learning.

What I have also learnt is that my comfort as a designer, and also from a studio-based model of teaching, in that I have been predisposed to enter comfortably in the transdisciplinary space. I now recognise that not everyone does so initially and with such ease, certainly from some disciplines where outcomes are more certain and the education is supported by decades of structured knowledge. Transdisciplinarity, by its collaborative nature, is more informal, less-structured and a less hierarchical model of educational and research engagement. It requires more than simply stepping on the boundaries of a disciplinary comfort zone. Spending time in the initial co-development, design and delivery of subjects and the confidence of staff to enter an unfamiliar environment of exploration was time well spent. Spending time with a wide range of these staff to develop an articulated co-understanding of methodologies across disciplines and co-created ways of working was similarly vital, with outcomes (curated packs of method cards for students) that still exist years later. What has become apparent is that, for the academic staff, this resulted in a level of refreshing engagement in creating educational design, curriculum and learning experiences within a new and fresh space. Highly involved and curious students have become like oxygen for the staff, with students and staff genuinely and collaboratively absorbed in the complexity of the challenges.

Having worked for 20 years within higher education in a disciplinary space, I now understand the luxury of working with significant numbers of students, all of whom wish to be there, with none undertaking their studies simply for the piece of paper or because university is unquestioned but not engaged with pathway.

They say that it takes a village to raise a child, but it takes a university to grow transdisciplinarity, and that will still take time. The expansion of research and establishing transdisciplinary research across the institution and through industry funding is still a challenging journey. Establishing a successful secondment programme for staff from across all other faculties has proved a similar challenge. In this, we need to clearly engage disciplines in seeing transdisciplinarity as not abandoning either the safety or the reputation of one's discipline behind but simply expanding upon it. Finding champions and creating participation in all parts of the university is vital and, in doing this, you need to be both persuader and manipulator. Working in a transdisciplinary space of educational development without the precedent that most more traditional university programmes build upon has been a challenge like no other, but one that generates and will generate many more outcomes than could be imagined.

GPSR Compliance

The European Union's (EU) General Product Safety Regulation (GPSR) is a set of rules that requires consumer products to be safe and our obligations to ensure this.

If you have any concerns about our products, you can contact us on

ProductSafety@springernature.com

In case Publisher is established outside the EU, the EU authorized representative is:

Springer Nature Customer Service Center GmbH
Europaplatz 3
69115 Heidelberg, Germany

www.ingramcontent.com/pod-product-compliance
Ingram Content Group UK Ltd.
Pitfield, Milton Keynes, MK11 3LW, UK
UKHW022232230426
12048UKWH00016BA/1212